What EVERY Church Should Know About Prison Ministry

A Study and Training Manual

By

Rev. Dr. Linda Lee Smith Barkman, PhD

Urban Loft Publishers | Skyforest, CA

What EVERY Church Should Know About Prison Ministry
A Study and Training Manual
Copyright © 2022 Barkman

Urban Loft Publishers
P.O. Box 6
Skyforest, CA 92385
www.urbanloftpublishers.com

Senior Editors: Stephen Burris & Kendi Howells Douglas
Copy Editor: Joel Ickes
Cover Design: Josh Walker
Interior Typesetting: Elisabeth Arnold & Amber Craft

ISBN-13: 978-1-949625-15-8

Made in the U.S

Dedication

This book is dedicated to:
Yaca Attwood,
Helen Waller,
Tom Hawkins,
and all the other prison ministry volunteers
who faithfully ministered Christ's love to me
both inside and outside prison.

Acknowledgements

This book is the result of collaborations on so many levels, and I am grateful for all of them. These are the people who ministered Christ's love to me while I was in prison. These are my prison brothers and sisters from whom I have learned so much. And then these are the individuals who supported me through the actual writing of this book.

Thank you to my mother, Alice Smith, who believes in me and the value of my work, and who listened for countless hours as I thought out loud about my drafts by talking with her on the phone.

Thank you to my favorite theology partner, my husband John, the other Dr. Barkman. His physical, emotional and spiritual support makes it possible for me to devote myself to this work. And he puts me back together when the memories of prison threaten to overwhelm me.

Thank you to Jarret Keith, who validated that my perspectives as a woman prisoner also resonate with my prison brothers.

Thank you to Good Shepherd Lutheran Church of Claremont, who accepted me into their midst just two weeks out of prison, and who have remained my role model of how a church can love a prisoner. And thank you to my godson Desmond, his brother Dietrich, and my compadres, Rev. Lara Martin and Rev. Rene Martin, who found a way to make us family indeed.

Thank you to Rev. Dr. Mandye Yates, and the First Christian Church Fullerton, who embraced my call, sponsored me in ordination, and were willing test subjects who participated in the first study from this book format.

I want to especially thank Joel Ickes, my thoughtful and thorough editor, whose encouragements, suggestions, corrections and questions were invaluable in bringing this book to completion.

Table of Contents

Chapter 6

Listen to Us! What Prisoners SAY That They Need........................83

Chapter 7

Theories of Prison Ministry: An Historical Perspective 93

Chapter 8

Prison Theology 101

Chapter 9

Forming a Contextual Theology of Prison Ministry 117

Chapter 10

A New Paradigm of Prison Ministry

Chapter 11

Complicating Issues 143

Chapter 12

What the Incarcerated Give Back (or What's in it for the Church?).......157

Conclusion

Tying Up Some Loose Ends...165

Bibliography 167

Introduction

An Insider's Perspective on Prison Ministry

The following are my unique set of credentials that qualify me to write this book. I was incarcerated at the California Institution for Women (CIW) in Chino, California, for 30 years. I was lay pastor to the prison psychiatric unit for 28 of those years. I hold a Master of Arts degree in Theology from Fuller Theological Seminary, most of which I earned through distance learning while still incarcerated. After leaving prison, I went on to earn a Ph.D. in Intercultural Studies from Fuller Theological Seminary, researching communication dynamics between prison ministry volunteers and incarcerated women. I am also an ordained minister with the Christian Church (Disciples of Christ).

In other words, I know prison ministry from the inside out.

It was the prison ministry volunteers I interviewed while doing my original research who first pleaded with me to write this book. They wanted to know how to do the vital work of bringing the gospel message to prisoners in the most effective ways possible. They wanted to know what it was that they were missing.

My formerly incarcerated sisters and brothers also asked me to write this book. They want the churches[1] to know what it is that prisoners do and do not need from them. The believers in prison desire to drink deeply from the well, but not all volunteers bring a bucket with them.

I hope to provide a handbook to help each church discover and develop its own callings and ministerial gifts. Along the way, churches will be challenged to think deeply about their own understanding of why they are doing what they do and where they intersect with mass incarceration issues in their contexts.

You will find discussion questions at the end of each chapter. I intend these questions to be thought-provoking, challenging, and equally valid for individual or group study. There are no wrong or right answers. In fact, your responses may well change as you continue to gain knowledge, experience, and understanding of the challenges associated with prison ministry.

A Little More About Me

I will take a little space here to share a few more autobiographic details to fill in the gaps from the terse first paragraph.[2] In 1979 I was 26 years old and had two young daughters, a two-year-old and a three-and-a-half-year-old. I was living with a physically abusive man who was not their father.

One tragic day, that man beat my two-year-old to death. At that time, California state law did not recognize Battered Woman Syndrome. Instead, although a jury found that I did not commit or aid and abet in the commission of bodily injury because I had not prevented him from killing my daughter, I was found guilty of second-degree murder. The specific rule used to convict me was *implied malice,* which meant that a rational person should have known what he was capable of doing, so I must have wanted him to do so, and the jury did not have to find that I was guilty of any malice. I was thus convicted and sentenced to 15-years-to-life in prison. He was

---

[1] Throughout this book, I will be making a distinction between "the Church" (with a capital "C") by which I mean the entire worldwide body of Christ, and "churches" (with a small "c") by which I am referring to the discrete bodies and individual buildings of various sizes and denominations.

[2] More details of my testimony can be found in an interview I did with M. Lee for *Christianity Today Magazine* in January 2019.

also convicted of second-degree murder (the appropriate sentence since he was not planning to commit murder) and sentenced to 15-years-to-life in prison, where he subsequently died in 2009. Current police attitudes suggest that no 26-year-old battered woman should be considered rational, and several detectives have apologized to me on behalf of their counterparts that I was ever arrested. Nevertheless, given the prevailing law and attitudes of the time, I was sent to the California Institution for Women in Chino, California, in July of 1980. That was my introduction to the then-budding phenomenon of mass incarceration.

In 1980, CIW was the only women's prison in California and was the world's largest women's prison. The population was just over 920. Currently, the population at CIW is almost 2000, and it is not even close to being the largest women's prison in the state. I ultimately served 30 years there and was released in August 2010. Why was I incarcerated so long on a 15-year sentence? It was due to the politicizing of paroles. It started when Dukakis was running for president. His campaign was derailed by TV ads saying, "Dukakis as governor of Massachusetts released Willie Horton from prison, and Horton murdered three more people. Is this who you want for president?" By 1988, a bill was passed in California giving the governor review and veto rights over the parole board. So even though I was found not to be a threat to society and was granted parole at my first hearing in 1989, that decision was ultimately overturned. Actually, I hold the record for all men and women doing life-term sentences in California. I was eventually **granted** parole 11 times, only to have it overturned the first ten times.

In the early years of my incarceration, in the 1980s, I studied for a Bachelor of Arts in Psychology/Human Development from the University of La Verne through extension classes, graduating in 1989 summa cum laude. After that, I worked in the prison's Mental Health Department as a Peer Helper (we could not be called Peer Counselors for legal reasons) for ten years. Then in 2005, Chaffey Community College began an Associate of Arts degree program which relied on prisoners who already had college degrees to work as tutors/facilitators for their classes, and I was hired as one of those original tutors. By this time, I was also working on a Certificate of Christian Study and later a Master's in Theology program from Fuller Theological Seminary.

I stayed sane through all of this by leaning on Jesus. I had much to learn as a babe in the Lord and a newbie to jail and prison. First of all, the volunteers who came into the county jail were very influential in helping me solidify my tenuous relationship with Jesus. They were lifesavers! When I arrived at CIW, some chaplains and volunteers provided services in the Reception Center and gave me hope. I desperately sought out opportunities to gather with God's people in church and Bible studies. Chaplains and prison ministry volunteers were lifelines to me. Soon, mainly because I played guitar, I became involved in leading worship.

For almost my entire incarceration from 1980 through 2010, I was closely involved with prison ministry volunteers. I was the appointed Inmate Moderator for the psychiatric unit, a position created by the Chaplain and recognized by prison staff. As such, I was responsible for meeting the volunteer ministry team as they entered the main yard, escorting them across the institution and through the gates and sally ports into the secure psychiatric unit. Some teams only used me as a worship leader with my guitar, while other teams sometimes insisted that I do a full share of the teaching. Either way, I spent several hours every week with these persons. And for almost a decade, the same teams and I would additionally provide services for both the prison hospital and the prison AIDS ward. Even during a two-year period when there were no volunteers available to the psychiatric unit and I was responsible for providing the entire Sunday services and midweek Bible studies, I was active in various services and Bible studies held for general population prisoners and led by outside volunteers. I am trying to communicate here the vast experience I have with the kind of prisoner-prison ministry relationships that I will discuss in this book.

I had been out of prison for three years, finished my master's degree work, and began my Ph.D. before realizing how important a book like this might be. I started my Ph.D. research convinced that I was most concerned with a prison-prisoner issue. I wanted to know what was happening with the women who found Christ in prison and made life-changing commitments to Jesus inside. We all know that recidivism is a huge issue, that too many prisoners return to prison upon release. But I wanted to understand why so many Christian women, women who were wholly dedicated to Jesus and confident that they were going to do well outside, not only came back but were so *excited* to come back to the church in prison. As an elder in the church, what was I doing wrong that so many women I discipled came back?

During the first year of Ph.D. seminars, I realized that the issue was not with the church at CIW. The church on the inside met all the criteria I was being taught as to what makes a thriving and viable mission church! I then began looking deeper into the relationships between women during and after prison with the churches outside. What I discovered then and since is providing the text of this book.

A Little Less About Me

My prison experience is that of an educated white woman, which is hardly the majority experience. Women make up only seven percent of the prison population. In good conscience, I cannot write this book without pushing against the inherent racism present in the structures and processes involved in mass incarceration.

This book is not primarily about racism, but prison is. Beginning with who is arrested, who is able to make bail, who can afford a private attorney, who is given the longest sentences, and who is provided resources upon release, non-white prisoners draw the short straw every time. And while this book is not primarily about racism, the power dynamics that underly and contribute to communication breakdowns are inextricably entwined with racist power issues. Therefore, throughout this book, I address racism as an underlying reality of mass incarceration, both implicitly and explicitly. This is my personal response to the deaths of George Floyd and so many other Black sisters and brothers that have occurred due to interactions with law enforcement.

How to Use This Workbook

This book is intended to be a practical workbook. For those who know nothing about prison or prison ministry, you will find introductory information in this comprehensive overview, supplemented by personal stories that open a window to life in one California women's prison. For those already active in prison ministry, you will find the prisoners' perspectives and hopefully be challenged to an even more effective ministry and outlook. For pastors, I have included several mini-sermons based on themes and scriptures that I have found particularly meaningful or helpful for prison ministry. For academic instructors and study leaders, there are study questions provided at the end of each chapter and endnotes. For students and study group members, you will find pages at the end of each chapter for your own notetaking. This book is organized to make it suitable for either a six- or 12-week study. I developed the Table of Contents order to flow and build on one another, whether chapters are assigned separately or in sequential pairs.

Discussion Questions

When you reach the conclusion of this book, you will revisit these questions. By answering them here, before you have read this book, and again when you have finished, you will be able to evaluate how the content of this book has informed your responses to the following questions.

1. Why do you believe that mass incarceration is a topic that is relevant to YOU?

2. What is your definition of prison ministry?

3. What is your understanding of power dynamics and your personal power?

4. What does prison ministry really look like from a Christian perspective?

5. How might God be calling you to participate in prison ministry?

Chapter 1

Why does EVERY Church need to know about Prison Ministry?

I realize that I am making a sweeping statement by titling this book, "What **Every** Church Should Know About Prison Ministry." You may well be thinking, "My little church doesn't do prison ministry. We are not located near a prison. I don't know of any of our members having anything to do with prison or jail. And we are already doing all the community outreach ministry that we have the resources to do." But I will make the case that mass incarceration and prison ministry are still topics relevant to you and your church even if all the above is true.

Who is affected by mass incarceration?

The truth is that no one in the United States is unaffected by mass incarceration. First of all, in the U.S., where our prison system costs taxpayers $80 billion per year (ACLU 2019), every taxpayer is affected in the pocketbook at the very least. You and your church are thus already involved in maintaining the system of mass incarceration.

The statistics about incarceration in the U.S. are absolutely staggering. Despite making up around five percent of the global population, the U.S. has nearly 25 percent of the world's prison population (ACLU). In a 2018 report, the Bureau of Justice Statistics stated that almost 2.2 *million* adults were being held in U.S. jails and prisons at the end of 2016 (Kahn 2019). According to the ACLU, that figure is now 2.3 *million*. If you can imagine the U.S. prison population as a single city, that city would be on the U.S.'s ten largest cities list. There are more people behind bars in America than living in major cities such as Philadelphia or Dallas (Kann 2019). And the problem is only growing. Since 1970, the incarcerated population of the US has increased by 700 percent, at a rate that has far outpaced population growth and crime (ACLU 2019).

The more conservative figure cited above of 2.2 million incarcerated adults also means that for every 100,000 people residing in the United States, approximately 655 of them were locked up (Kahn 2019). But to make that figure more personally relevant, let's break it down into more manageable numbers. The significance becomes more immediate when that figure is translated down to at least six out of every thousand Americans is incarcerated. Let's take it even further; at least one of every two hundred Americans is currently in prison or jail.

But mass incarceration does not only affect the people who are behind bars. Remember that each of these incarcerated persons has family, friends, and/or victims outside prison. A study from 2015 found that 44 percent of Black women and 12 percent of white women have a family member imprisoned, which means that about one in four women in the United States currently has a family member in prison (Lee et al, 2015). It is simply not reasonable to think that any church is unaffected. This has not always been the case. When I was arrested in 1980, I did not know anyone who had ever been to prison. The same was true for most of my friends. However, this is no longer our reality in the U.S.

Invariably, no matter how small the audience is when I speak about incarceration, someone approaches me with a story about a family member or friend who has been, or currently is, behind bars. It is very common that it is the very person in front of me who was in jail or prison. People are more likely to share their stories because I am open about my own previous incarceration. They have some assurance that I will accept them rather than judge them. These people are already sitting in the pews of your churches, but you are likely to be unaware of their connection to mass incarceration.

It should be no surprise that exactly *who* is being incarcerated varies by demographics. While mass incarceration affects everyone, African Americans are disproportionately affected. Race is an issue that permeates the structures responsible for and active in mass incarceration. In 2017, only 5.6 percent of California's male adult residents were in prison, while 28.5 percent of California's male prisoners were African American. For African American males, the imprisonment rate is ten times that of white men (Harris et al 2019). The same discrepancy holds true for women, where 5.7 percent of California's adult women were imprisoned, but 25.9 percent of female prisoners were African American.

One out of every three African American male babies born today can expect to go to prison in his lifetime, as can one of every six Latino males, compared to a rate of only one of every 17 white boys (ACLU 2019). Furthermore, according to a report by the Hamilton Project, "There is nearly a 70 percent chance that an African American man without a high school diploma will be imprisoned by his mid-thirties" (Kearney et al 2014).

At the current rate, if not our own sons, almost certainly some of our sons' schoolmates will spend time incarcerated. And while women make up only about seven percent of those incarcerated in the U.S., women are the fastest-growing segment of the incarcerated population in several categories, such as suspensions and law enforcement referrals. Further, the disparities between Black and white girls eclipse those between Black and white boys (Green, Walker & Shapiro 2020).

Many of those who have been constrained behind bars have never committed or been convicted of a crime. There are twice as many people sitting in jails awaiting trial and presumed innocent as there are in the entire federal prison system. Many of them will indeed be acquitted and then released. And then there are people, like my dear friend Gloria, who, although initially convicted, are ultimately exonerated.[3]

---

[3] Gloria was originally tried as a death penalty case, was eventually sentenced to 25 years to life in prison, and after 17 years was exonerated. You can read her account in *Full Circle: A True Story of Murder, Lies, and Vindication* by Gloria Killian and Sandra Kobrin, 2012, New Horizon Press, Far Hills, NJ.

Another astounding statistic is that 650,000 men and women nationwide return from prison to their communities each year. In fact, most people who are jailed or incarcerated are eventually released. Then comes the immense challenge of making (or remaking) on the outside. They face nearly 50,000 federal, state, and local legal restrictions that make it difficult to reintegrate back into society (ACLU 2019). These people are our neighbors, whether you are aware of them or not, and assuring that they are able to adjust to life outside prison walls is in our own best interests. It is part of keeping neighborhoods safe and being a humanitarian response to those in need of support.

This means that *your* church is already somehow involved with the problem and is, therefore, called to be part of the answer. It is likely than you suspect that you have some church members who have personally experienced jail or prison. It is even more likely that you have church members who have family or friends who are currently in or have been in prison or jail. And just as importantly, you may well have church members who have been the victims of crime. And there is no getting around the fact that most of your church members are taxpayers who thus have a say in making decisions about prisons and punishments.

Most prisoners are eventually released. In an interview held shortly before her retirement as the Warden at the California Institution for Women in December of 2009, Dawn Davison explained, "It's my duty to take these women for the time that they're here and give them what they can to get better so they'll one day get out. They're presumptive citizens in here"(Davison, Jenness and Lynch 2011). Unfortunately, Davison's attitude that women prisoners are presumptive citizens was not shared by political powers or her successors. [4]

One unintended but real benefit of mass incarceration is reducing the stigma attached to the label "prisoner." Even the famous and wealthy are included in mass incarceration statistics. TV stars such as Lori Loughlin and Felicity Huff face jail or prison time in the college entrance scandal. Martha Stewart served her federal prison sentence and then returned to her television show no worse for the wear.

---

[4] This attitude of Davidson's, that the prisoners in her care were humans who deserved respect, was pervasive during her tenure as Warden.

Expanding Our Definition of Prison Ministry

We need to develop a working definition of prison ministry for this book by expanding preconceived notions that limit its scope. Prison ministry covers a much broader spectrum than you are probably thinking. Even our Quaker predecessors in prison reform intended the entire carceral experience to be ministry, a topic addressed in depth in Chapter 7. There is much more to prison ministry than leading worship or Bible study within a prison or jail, although these are essential aspects. Just as mass incarceration affects a larger population and is more inherently racist than most people in the U.S. are aware of, ministering to those impacted by mass incarceration is a more expansive enterprise than most people imagine.

First, we need to understand how many types of facilities are involved in prison-related containment of individuals. In addition to federal prisons, state prisons, and county or city jails, some people are contained within juvenile facilities and ICE detention centers. Halfway houses, reentry programs, and even mental hospitals house prisoners who need spiritual care. Each and every one of these facilities is a mission field and provides a nexus for introducing people to the love and care of Jesus Christ.

Prison or Jail? There is a difference!

The terms prison and jail are not interchangeable! The uninitiated often confuse them, while people who are locked up are very aware of the differences. County and city jails, state prisons, and federal prisons each hold distinctly different populations and are subject to totally different rules, regulations, and oversight.

Jail generally refers to a municipal locked facility (city- or county-operated) where people are held for specific reasons. Primarily, jails are where persons are held after arrest but before being convicted of a crime and sentenced. Thus, many people in jail have never been, and will never be, convicted of a crime. Persons who are ultimately convicted of misdemeanors and minor felonies that result in sentences of a year or less then serve their time in jails.

However, those convicted of a serious felony are remanded to prisons. Some judges actually impose sentences of "a year and a day" to ensure that persons will serve their sentence in a state prison rather than county jail. While jails are intended to be short-term lock-up facilities, the reality is that the trial process can take up to several years, especially for those tried for grave crimes.

Occasionally, state prisoners (and sometimes even federal prisoners) will be held in county jails for brief periods. The two most likely reasons for this are child custody hearings and appeals to the court. In these circumstances, state prisoners find themselves in the county jail closest to the court at which they will be appearing. Some state and federal prisoners have never been to jail. These prisoners are more likely to be white and/or have adequate financial means for posting bail. As a result, these persons are sometimes allowed the privilege of turning themselves in ot the state or federal prison to which they are sentenced and bypassing the uncomfortable and demeaning experience of "jail."

Strangely enough, many prisons have a "jail" lock-up facility where prisoners are detained while being investigated and adjucated for crimes or rules infractions that occur within the prison.

But prison ministry must extend beyond the walls of containment facilities. Those who are leaving those facilities still need care. Returning citizens need both resources and spiritual help. And as someone who left prison ten years ago at this writing, I can assure you that these needs continue long after release. After the acute needs are dealt with in the first days, weeks, and months, incarceration leaves scars and wounds that need to be tended for years.

Additionally, prison ministry must include the needs of those who are not themselves locked up but who are severely impacted by the incarceration of another. First amongst these must be the children left behind. Children whose parents are incarcerated often suffer greatly; emotionally, spiritually, and financially (Bernstein 2005). But the trauma often extends to spouses, parents, siblings, and others whose lives are in turmoil as the result of the imprisonment of a loved one.

Another overlooked area of prison ministry involves the needs of the victims of crime. Restorative justice programs, spiritual help for those who are traumatized by crime, and support of those who incur terrible losses due to crime should also be considered part of prison ministry.

Public education about the crisis of mass incarceration also has its place within the spectrum of prison ministry. Through educational programs, our church members can affect the systems and structures of mass incarceration through informed voting. In a 2016 study by the Brennan Center which examined the convictions and sentences of 1.46 million people behind bars, they found that 39 percent, over half a million people, were locked up for nonviolent crimes that did not constitute a public safety issue (Cullen 2018). Community service programs could and should therefore also have a place under the umbrella of prison ministry.

Biblical Mandate for Prison Ministry

The church has a clear biblical mandate for prison ministry. But I contend that this mandate does not come from the scripture that you are probably thinking of. Many Christians think first of Jesus' words, "I was in prison and you visited me" (Matthew 25:36b). While this does point the church towards prison, I think that to base prison ministry on this verse alone is a mistake (a topic I will discuss at length in Chapter 2 of this book). There are even stronger biblical reasons for every church to be informed about and involved in prison ministry.

The Matthew 22:37-40 giving of the great commandment is one of these stronger arguments.

> *'You shall love the Lord your God with all your heart, and with all your soul, and with all your mind.' This is the greatest and first commandment. And a second is like it: 'You shall love your neighbor as yourself.' On these two commandments hang all the law and the prophets. (NRSV)*

The issue here is that number of prisoners in the U.S. is just too great. We can no longer deny that the incarcerated are our neighbors simply because we have removed them from the rest of society and shut them away. At one time, there were few enough prisoners, and they were locked up far enough away (prisons are usually intentionally built in remote areas) that it was possible to forget about them. But media coverage of mass incarceration in the U.S. makes forgetting the prisoner impossible. The issue of mass incarceration has permeated our entire society.

In the parable of the Good Samaritan in Luke 10, Jesus explains to us what it means to love our neighbors; it is to show them "mercy" (Luke 10:37). In the parable, fear and disgust concerning the wounded and naked man in the ditch caused religious leaders to walk around him. After all, that man in the ditch might be a dangerous criminal, right? However, even if some people assert that dangerous criminals have forfeited their status as neighbors, how can the church justify ignoring their innocent families and victims?

Here is another verse that challenges us to prison ministry. The prophet asks us in Micah 6:8, "What does the Lord require of you but to do justice, and to love kindness, and to walk humbly with your God?" I am not going to argue whether or not incarceration is justice. But given that our judicial system sends people to prison, is it justice to leave them behind bars without ministering to their souls? I suspect that $80 billion per year paid by taxpayers to support our prison system could be better spent building up, not further harming, communities. Investment, not incarceration, is how we can best improve safety.

Discussion Questions

1. Which statistic did you find most surprising regarding mass incarceration? Why was this surprising?

2. Why is it important to understand the difference between jails and prisons?

3. Do you know people who have been in jail or prison? How does this affect your perceptions about prison ministry?

4. Why should YOUR church know about prison ministry?

5. What additional scriptures can you think of that provide a biblical mandate for prison ministry? What do these scriptures tell you about God's position about prisoners?

6. What is your reason for reading this book? What are you personally hoping to get from reading it?

Chapter 2

A Biblical Perspective on Crime and Prisoners

When I first began researching the topic of prison ministry, I discovered that one major common thread in academic literature advocating or discussing prison ministry is the use of Matthew 25:36b as a foundational scripture (Vargas 2013, LaHurd 2013, Pounder 2008, Levad 2011, McBride 2014, Nelson 2013, et al). I agree that when Jesus says, "I was in prison, and you visited me," it is indeed a direct reference to both Jesus and to prisoners. However, to stand on this one scripture as foundational to prison ministry is problematic. I will spend some time on this issue here for a crucial reason: while hospitality is a vital need in prison ministry that is too often overlooked, it is **not** sufficient to explain the need for prison ministry. Further, if the basis of a ministry is hospitality, then the redemption needs of a large portion of prisoners are liable to be overlooked or neglected.

Two main issues arise when prison ministry is based primarily on Matthew 25:36. The first issue has to do with the kinds of people that Jesus is referring to. I will be making the case that the prisoners that Jesus is referring to are not guilty criminals who have been convicted of violent or injurious crimes, but instead are innocent debtors and political prisoners. The second issue is that what Jesus is mandating in Matthew 25:36 is a ministry of hospitality, and while the church must obey this command to extend hospitality even to prisoners, the foundational principle of prison ministry must be Christ's redemptive work on the cross which extends even to guilty criminals. Let's take a closer look at each of these issues in turn.

Innocent prisoners vs. guilty criminals:

There are actually three categories of prisoners that need to be addressed for a comprehensive understanding of prison ministry. However, Matthew 25:36b is only relevant to, at most, two of them. The three categories are: (1) the totally innocent, (2) the innocent due to mitigating circumstances, and (3) the guilty. So, while the first two may well be generally regarded as deserving of the hospitality that Jesus refers to in Matthew 25:36, an argument can be made, and often is made, that there is justification to exclude the guilty criminal from this sort of ministry. A closer look will show that all who are imprisoned are needing and deserving of our attention in prison ministry.

Totally innocent: There are people in prisons and jails that are totally innocent of any crime or criminal behavior. Jesus was an innocent prisoner, pronounced so by Pontius Pilate (John 18:38). Jesus had committed no crime worthy of punishment, and yet was flogged and incarcerated… until His execution. The apostle Paul was likewise imprisoned for political and religious reasons (Acts 25:25)… until his ultimate execution.

Many people believe that everyone in prison or jail deserves to be there. I had forgotten this assumption but had it reinforced to me recently. A young man wanted to witness Christ to me after we recently met on a neighborhood hiking trail, asking me if I was saved. Upon hearing my answer that not only am I a believer, but also that I am actively involved in prison ministry, he exclaimed, "Oh! I guess there must be people in prison who don't really deserve to be there and need ministry!" It had never occurred to him that there might be innocent people in prison. So, although he was actively evangelizing strangers walking in his path, he had never thought about the need for prison ministry. And he still was not conceptualizing that people who were not innocent were deserving of ministry and God's grace.

Modern examples of this kind of innocent prisoner include Nelson Mandela and Martin Luther King Jr., both of whom may have violated the letter of the law, but did so because they were fighting unjust laws, with moral reasons, and for the greater good of others. Most people have no problem with the idea of visiting such persons in prison and ministering to their needs. I maintain that these are the prisoners that Jesus is primarily referring to in Matthew 25:36, deserving of the church's hospitality.

I further maintain that it is a stretch, and not very helpful, to equate and apply the writings of Dr. Martin Luther King Jr. from Birmingham Jail to the average, not-so-innocent prisoner. I realized the necessity of making this point when I was invited to guest speak to a group about exactly this since they were studying the book of Acts and were comparing King's "Letter from Birmingham Jail" to the writings of Paul from prison. (Why I do not consider Paul an innocent prisoner will be discussed later in this chapter.) However, as 1 Peter 2:20 explains, "If you endure when you are beaten for doing wrong, what credit is that? But if you endure when you do right and suffer for it, you have God's approval."

Innocent due to mitigating circumstances: A related category consists of those perceived as having been wrongly convicted of a crime, or for whom strong mitigating circumstances exist. The theologian Dietrich Bonhoeffer, who was imprisoned until his execution for the crime of attempting to assassinate Adolph Hitler, is one prime example of this category of prisoner. I share the deep regard with which Bonhoeffer is widely held, and acknowledge the relevance of his theological insights. However, as with Martin Luther King Jr., it is a grave error to treat Bonhoeffer as a typical prisoner. One difference is that while innocent prisoners and those with mitigating circumstances have experienced the dehumanizing effects of incarceration, they do not experience the depth of guilt and shame that is part of the carceral experience of guilty prisoners. Further, innocent prisoners and those with mitigating circumstances are perceived to present a different type of threat to society at large than guilty prisoners do.

Women who kill their abusers are another example of prisoners who are often perceived to fall into this second category. As intimate partner violence is becoming better understood, prisoners who were victims of this type of abuse are more often understood as worthy of compassion and ministry. I am frequently regarded as belonging to this category, although I relate more to the next category.

The guilty criminal: Strangely overlooked in many discussions of prison ministry is the category of the guilty criminal. This is a category of prisoners who have, for whatever reason, actually committed such crimes as theft, robbery, assault, or murder. These are crimes that create victims, crimes that understandably frighten and concern members of society, including members of our churches. Yet, in truth, most prisoners serving sentences in the U.S. have in fact participated in such crimes.

The question then becomes whether these prisoners are redeemable and worthy of ministry. Although some believe that most prisoners are morally vicious, my experience is that the majority of even these guilty criminals are looking for a way to redemption. Further, even the morally vicious are in desperate need of Christ, whether or not they are willing to receive him.

I do not say this lightly. The man who actually killed my daughter was ultimately diagnosed as narcissistic, sociopathic, and not a good candidate for therapy. I am comforted that he spent the rest of his life in prison, where he was less able to do harm to others. Nevertheless, I maintain that he was also created in the *imago dei,* in the image of God, and needed to hear the gospel message of hope.

Hospitality vs. redemption as a foundational precept: So why do I maintain that hospitality as a foundation for prison ministry is not adequate by itself? Although prisoners are given special mention in the Bible, they do not fall under the same umbrella as orphans, widows, and strangers. In Matthew 25:36b, Jesus emphasizes the Old Testament themes of caring for the orphan, widow, and stranger[5] by meeting their needs for food, water, clothing, shelter, and medical care. However, Matthew 25:36b does not address the underlying issues the church faces today in dealing with imprisoned criminals and their reentry into society. While

------

[5] I give grateful acknowledgment to the distinguished Old Testament theologian Walter Brueggemann for helping me achieve this insight. In his Fuller Forum lectures at Fuller Theological Seminary on May 1, 2015, Brueggemann repeatedly emphasized the Old Testament importance of care and hospitality for the widow, the orphan, and the stranger. As I considered his arguments, it became increasingly clear to me that he was correct in omitting the prisoner, changing my entire mindset about prison ministry.

hospitality to prisoners and ex-prisoners is a necessary component of prison ministry, hospitality is not the appropriate *foundation* for the Christian response to the physical, emotional, and spiritual needs of persons incarcerated for crimes. Prison ministry teams who lead worship services in prisons will be crippled if what they are offering goes no deeper than a helping hand of hospitality. Likewise, churches will be significantly hindered in ministering to released prisoners and accepting them in their midst if their members have not been helped to surmount their own fears, prejudices, and traumas related to crime and criminals. Yet, as we discussed in the previous chapter, the magnitude of mass incarceration in the U.S. is such that the church must be part of the solution.

Unless churches recognize that even guilty prisoners number among the redeemable, hospitality only serves as an instrument for keeping these prisoners at arm's length (Nelson 2013, 94). According to the Miriam Webster On-line Dictionary, hospitality is defined as the "generous and friendly treatment of visitors and guests" (2015). What this means is that hospitality always, by definition, creates a wall between those who belong to the household and the 'other' to whom hospitality is extended. Maintaining the 'otherness' of prisoners is not an effective technique for helping prisoners re-orient towards the norms of the society from which they are isolated, and certainly does not assist prisoners in the process of reintegration upon release from prison.

Communion

I do not think there are words that adequately describe what happened within my soul and spirit the first time my pastor asked me to serve as communion assistant, what it meant that a pastor and congregation saw fit to allow this former prisoner, still on parole, to share the cup of blessing with each and every member of our church!

During my incarceration, for many reasons, communion was offered very sparingly. My last decade in prison, our chaplain was concerned that the women I ministered to in the psychiatric unit did not possess the capability to make informed decisions about taking communion. Thus, to prevent these prisoners from "eating the bread or drinking the cup of the Lord in an unworthy manner" and becoming "answerable for the body and blood of the Lord" (1 Cor. 11:27), communion was not offered there. Since I was leading those services, which were concurrent with any communion services at the main chapel, I missed out on communion. And since the Catholic chaplain at the time was a nun and not a priest, only the wafer was offered to our Catholic sisters at mass. These experiences meant that joining my sisters and brothers in communion at church was exceptionally meaningful. But the first time my pastor asked me to serve as lay communion assistant, knowing that I was on parole at that time, this gave me an entirely new perspective of what it means to be fully integrated into Christ's body.

In the following section, as we study what the Bible says about prisoners, we will ultimately discover that while Jesus extends hospitality even to sinners and criminals, he does not stop at hospitality. Jesus restores criminals to community and, further, he welcomes criminals into the intimacy of his household. These examples of integration are what the church is called to emulate in prison ministry.

To understand what real prison ministry is about, we should carefully study what scripture says about crime and criminals. The differences between the justice systems in the ancient Near East and what we see in the U.S. today are profound.

Crime and Criminals in the Old Testament

There are numerous accounts given in Old Testament scripture of the types of crimes for which people in the U.S. are now routinely incarcerated. A close examination reveals that these historic crimes are dealt with far differently than what we are accustomed to reading about in our newspapers.

Let us begin by examining what the Old Testament reveals about the crime we call murder. Cain is the original, prototypical murderer in the Bible.

8 Cain said to his brother Abel, "Let us go out to the field." And when they were in the field, Cain rose up against his brother Abel, and killed him. 9 Then the Lord said to Cain, "Where is your brother Abel?" He said, "I do not know; am I my brother's keeper?" 10 And the Lord said, "What have you done? Listen; your brother's blood is crying out to me from the ground! 11 And now you are cursed from the ground, which has opened its mouth to receive your brother's blood from your hand. 12 When you till the ground, it will no longer yield to you its strength; you will be a fugitive and a wanderer on the earth." 13 Cain said to the Lord, "My punishment

Using contemporary judicial language, Cain committed violence against his own brother, and there is evidence of malice aforethought. A previous verse (v. 5) describes Cain as "very angry" before taking Abel out to the field, making this a first-degree murder case. Cain then tried to deny that he had killed his brother. This refusal to take responsibility is something else a modern court would hold against him. However, this case was not adjudicated in court but by God himself. We then read in this account that Cain was not given the death penalty; he was not even imprisoned! Further, Cain was marked by God in order to protect Cain from those who would do him hurt. What might God be trying to tell us through his example here? Perhaps more examples will make the answer to this question clearer.

Moses, who is credited with writing/compiling the first five books of the Bible, also committed murder.

11 One day, after Moses had grown up, he went out to his people and saw

their forced labor. He saw an Egyptian beating a Hebrew, one of his

kinsfolk. 12 He looked this way and that, and seeing no one he killed the

Egyptian and hid him in the sand. 13 When he went out the next day, he

saw two Hebrews fighting; and he said to the one who was in the wrong,

"Why do you strike your fellow Hebrew?" 14 He answered, "Who made

you a ruler and judge over us? Do you mean to kill me as you killed the

Egyptian?" Then Moses was afraid and thought, "Surely the thing is

known." (Ex. 2:11-14)

The biblical account says that Moses looked around, and seeing no witnesses, killed an Egyptian and buried him in the sand. It is unclear whether this was another premeditated murder or a crime of passion and opportunity, which would be termed second-degree murder in a modern court. That he was coming to the defense of someone else might be mildly mitigating, might provide a partial excuse for his behavior. Still, it would not exonerate him from responsibility for the death. All this notwithstanding, decades later, when God heard the cries of his oppressed people, he appeared to Moses in the burning bush and commissioned Moses to lead the Hebrew people (Ex. 3). Fascinatingly, it was ultimately Moses the murderer who is charged with bringing God's ten commandments to the people, including the commandment, "You shall not murder" (Ex. 20:13, Deut. 5:17).

King David, described as a man after God's own heart, was also a murderer (2 Sam. 11:1-27). Moreover, according to current California law, he would have qualified for the "special circumstances" that can lead to either the death penalty or life-without-parole sentences. Verse 15 informs us that, in the letter he wrote, King David ordered Joab to "Set Uriah in the forefront of the hardest fighting, and then draw back from him, so that he may be struck down and die." This is hard evidence for having premeditated, conspired, and masterminded the plot that resulted in Uriah's death.

While there are many accounts of people in the Old Testament committing murder, the surprising fact is that none of these murderers are imprisoned for their crimes. How God deals with each is, instead, dependent upon how each person relates to the crime and to God when confronted by their deeds. I am **not** excusing murder; please understand me. Murder is a grievous sin against God and persons that causes immeasurable pain and grief for all concerned and for which there are grave consequences. However, in these biblical accounts, the consequence was not imprisonment.

Neither does the Old Testament deal with the crimes of theft and stealing by imposing prison sentences upon the guilty. Instead, God demands restitution (Ex. 22). Those who cannot pay the restitution may then be put in debtors' prison or even sold as a slave, but this consequence is for being unable to pay the debt, not actually for stealing. After all, Proverbs declares, "Thieves are not despised who steal only to satisfy their appetite when they are hungry" (Prov. 6:30).

On the other hand, most of what the Old Testament defines as crime carries the death penalty. Exodus 21-22 and Leviticus 20 name death as the necessary consequence of the following: murder, striking one's parents, kidnapping, cursing one's parents, lying with an animal, profaning the Sabbath, adultery, male homosexuality, and wizardry. In California today, of this list, only murder, kidnapping, and assault (striking a parent) are even felonies.

Paradoxically, Old Testament prisoners are usually innocent of anything that would be accounted crime in the U.S. today. The first mention of the word 'prison' in the Bible has to do with the false imprisonment of Joseph for a rape he never attempted or committed (Gen 39:20). And those who were imprisoned with him, the pharaoh's cupbearer and baker, were both there for having offended Pharaoh (Gen. 40:1). Samson killed people, and was imprisoned, but the explanation is given that Samson was God's instrument to deliver Israel from the Philistines. In other words, this was an act of war (Judges 14:4). The prophet Micaiah was imprisoned for giving an unpopular prophecy to the king (1 Kings 22:26-27, 2 Chron. 18:26). The prophet Hanani, likewise, was detained for displeasing the king (2 Chron. 16:10). King Jehoiachin was a political prisoner of Babylon (2 Kings 24:12). The prophet Jeremiah was wrongly imprisoned for the false charge of desertion (Jer. 37:14). Finally, the book of Psalms mentions God setting free prisoners "who were doomed to die" (Ps. 120:20), but there is no evidence that the prisoners spoken of were anything but the same kind of innocent political prisoners I have been describing (Ps. 79:11, 107:10, 142:7, 146:7).

While this is not an exhaustive study of the Old Testament and crime, these scriptures support my position that the prisoners Jesus refers to in Matthew 25:36 do not fit the category of guilty criminals. Now we will look at what the New Testament has to say about crime and criminals.

Crime and criminals in the New Testament

1 Corinthians 6:9-11 gives us a laundry list of behaviors that prevent entry into the kingdom of God. This list includes items easily recognizable as crimes for which people are now incarcerated, such as theft and robbery. Also listed are behaviors such as greed and drunkenness, which can be contextualized and translated

as consistent with the more modern drug abuse and trafficking crimes. Yet Paul explicitly states that the believers he addresses in this epistle were formerly just such criminals who are now washed, sanctified, and justified in Christ. Moreover, Paul refers to himself in 1 Timothy 1:8-16 as "formerly a blasphemer, a persecutor, and a man of violence" who received mercy, and this precisely so he would become an example of what Jesus Christ can do in the lives of sinners.

The writer of Ephesians 4:22-28 specifically addresses thieves as being amongst those who are taught to put away the former corrupt life and to clothe themselves "with the new self, created according to the likeness of God in true righteousness and holiness." So former thieves are acceptably integrated within the body of Christ. This is a strong argument for sharing the gospel of Jesus with criminals, for recognizing that such are considered redeemable by God, and for fully receiving those who accept Christ into the family of God.

How does Jesus interact with criminals in the Gospels?

As we have seen so far, there is much to be gleaned from a diligent search of scripture for examples and instruction concerning crime and criminals. I hold the perspective that nothing in scripture should be more authoritative to the church than the words and actions of Jesus himself. Thus, it is extremely valuable for us to examine the gospels from the perspective of Jesus as our teacher. We will now take a closer look at the teachings of Jesus, while paying close attention to the historical context of his ministry to determine what guidance Jesus offers for an embodied and contextual understanding of criminals (Williams 2013).

Zacchaeus: Luke 19:1-10 gives us the story of the crooked tax collector Zacchaeus and his encounter with Jesus.

> *He entered Jericho and was passing through it. 2 A man was there named Zacchaeus; he was a chief tax collector and was rich. 3 He was trying to see who Jesus was, but on account of the crowd he could not, because he was short in stature. 4 So he ran ahead and climbed a sycamore tree to see him, because he was going to pass that way. 5 When Jesus came to the place, he*

looked up and said to him, "Zacchaeus, hurry and come down; for I must stay at your house today." 6 So he hurried down and was happy to welcome him. 7 All who saw it began to grumble and said, "He has gone to be the guest of one who is a sinner." 8 Zacchaeus stood there and said to the Lord, "Look, half of my possessions, Lord, I will give to the poor; and if I have defrauded anyone of anything, I will pay back four times as much." 9 Then Jesus said to him, "Today salvation has come to this house, because he too is a son of Abraham. 10 For the Son of Man came to seek out and to save the lost." (NRSV)

This text is so rich that I cannot resist giving this character a rather in-depth treatment. First, to understand Zacchaeus better, think of him as more a "collector for the mob" than a "respectable and law-abiding IRS agent" (Anderson 1997). Most significant for our study are the following points:

1. *Zacchaeus was looking for Jesus.* Like many other criminals, Zacchaeus was not content or at peace with his life. Despite his unsavory lifestyle and means of support, this man was actively seeking Jesus.

2. *Jesus saw him* and stated that He "must stay at [Zacchaeus'] house today." Jesus picked him out of a crowd. Admittedly, a short man in rich man's clothing perched up in a tree is not an everyday sight. But still, instead of being overlooked, Zacchaeus was asked to extend hospitality to Jesus.

3. *Zacchaeus repents.* Zacchaeus made life-changing public repentance of his crimes. Further, he not only promised to divest himself of ill-gotten gains, he vowed to pay double the restitution required by Old Testament law.

4. *Jesus accepts Zacchaeus back into community.* "Today salvation has come to this house" (Luke 19:9). Jesus **fully** restores Zacchaeus back into community. He is not simply a marginalized former criminal, but Jesus declares him to be restored as a son of Abraham.

5. *Jesus explains that He came to seek out and save the lost.* **This** is a precedent for prison ministry. Jesus did not shy away from the guilty criminal, but instead intentionally visited him in his home. And as a result of the visit and his spiritual and ethical turnaround, Zacchaeus is assured of salvation.

The woman taken in adultery: John 8:1-11, the account of the woman taken in adultery, provides us more insight into how Jesus views criminals. The significant points are that:

1. The woman had been caught in the act and was absolutely guilty,
2. Adultery was, at that time, a capital offense (Lev. 20:10),
3. While Jesus does not defend the guilty criminal, he points to the guilty hearts of all who would accuse her,
4. Jesus speaks his refusal to condemn her, and ultimately,
5. Jesus rescues her from the consequences of her past sin and enjoins her against future sin.

There is no discussion of possible mitigating circumstances that might make her crime more palatable. But neither is the woman referred to by name in a way that would immortalize her shame. Instead, Jesus restores her to her community.

Thief on the cross: The thief on the cross next to Jesus is another important indicator of Jesus' position towards criminals (Luke 23:41-44). He is traditionally referred to as Saint Dismus or San Dimas. This scripture tells us that the thief who feared God:

1. acknowledged his own sin,
2. confessed the innocence of Jesus,
3. called on Jesus as sovereign, and
4. was promised to join Jesus in paradise that very day.

In this case, Jesus did not deliver the criminal from the worldly penalty for his crimes. However, Jesus assures the thief of membership within the community of the Spirit in paradise.

Sermonette: Luke 23:42

> Then he said, "Jesus, remember me when you come into your kingdom."
> (Luke 23:42)

A goodly number of theologians have explored the tension between Christ's reign having begun and Christ's reign to be completed at the eschaton/end times. But something less often explored in North America is what it means for Jesus to "come into" his kingdom. My expanded understanding comes from, of all places, watching subtitled Korean historical dramas. An often-repeated theme in these historical dramas is that of a usurped throne, and of a surviving heir of the original king struggling to claim his rightful place on the throne. The rightful heir is then supported in his struggles by those righteous people who believe in him. The trusted companions who are with the heir when he achieves his throne and comes into his kingdom are greatly rewarded; they become the most powerful of the leaders. Those companions who sacrifice their lives in the struggle ask the heir to "remember me when you come into your kingdom," which the heir does by providing for the families of the fallen supporters.

There is a reason that supporting the rightful heir, especially when he seems to be too weak to overthrow the usurper, deserves such special honor. Just as it is when said by the thief crucified on the cross next to Jesus, asking to be remembered when the heir "comes into" his kingdom is a statement of incredible faith.

Barabbas: Barabbas is described in the gospels as a bandit (John 18:40) who was "in prison for an insurrection that had taken place in the city, and for murder" (Luke 23:19). Thus, a murderer, Barabbas, was set free and restored to the community who called out for him while the innocent Son of God, Jesus, was crucified. I find it fascinating that there is no hint or intimation in Scripture that Barabbas was grateful to either Jesus or God due to his release. Furthermore, there is no reference to Barabbas repenting of his crimes and sins. Nevertheless, Jesus gave his life for the freedom of this prisoner.

Matthew: There is one more gospel account of someone whose interactions with Jesus are particularly significant to our purposes in this chapter. Matthew was another tax collector and collaborator with the foreign occupiers, who:

1. is called to follow Jesus,
2. with other "tax collectors and sinners" dines with Jesus (Matt. 9:9-13), and
3. is later named as an apostle (Matt. 10:3, Luke 6:15).

Far beyond the hospitality of dining with Matthew, Jesus eradicates the barrier of "other" by bringing Matthew into intimate relationship, into his household.

Saul/Paul: This next example describes an encounter with Jesus occurring after his crucifixion and death. In other words, the account in Acts 9:1-22 of the conversion of Saul of Tarsus is an example of how the *resurrected* Christ relates to criminals. Saul begins, in this narrative, "breathing threats and murder" (9:1), even if doing so within the confines of the existing law of the land. Yet we must surely judge this behavior to be not only criminal but what we would classify a "hate crime," in that he intended this harm against the Church. I dare say that the closest parallels we have to Saul's persecution of the church might be those tragic church shooters that have made headlines in recent years or those Christians who participated in rounding up Jews during the Holocaust. These examples are harsh, but unless we understand the enormity of Saul's crime, we cannot grasp the enormity of Jesus' fantastic response. Jesus confronts Saul, reveals himself to Saul, heals Saul, disciples Saul, and brings Saul into community in the Church. Jesus' work in Saul extends so far that a new person with a new identity, the apostle Paul, is the result.

Hermeneutic – what we learn from Jesus' example:

Jesus does not excuse crime. Instead, Jesus forgives criminals. And although Jesus indeed extends hospitality even to sinners and criminals, he does not stop at hospitality. Jesus restores criminals to community and even welcomes criminals into the intimacy of his household.

Discussion Questions

1. What is the most difficult concept about the Bible and criminals for you to embrace? Why?

2. Can you think of any other criminals or incarcerated people in the Bible? How are they presented?

3. What do you think about Saul's crime and Jesus' response?

4. How well do you think the Church is doing at restoring criminals to community? What could be done differently?

5. Why is it important to understand that not all prisoners are guilty, and that not all prisoners are innocent? How does this make prison ministry more challenging?

Chapter 3

Muted Group Theory – Power Dynamics and Prisoners

These next two chapters will focus on two theories that help describe power dynamics in communication and how these dynamics are relevant to prison ministry. This chapter is an introduction to Muted Group Theory (MGT). MGT describes how relative power explains and affects how we communicate with each other in broad terms. Chapter 4 will follow up by looking more specifically at how these communication dynamics impact and influence those who minister and those who are ministered to.

My own introduction to MGT was not initially remarkable. I noticed it in a brief paragraph hidden within the Gender Communications chapter in a college textbook and cited it in a paper. At the time, I was looking for an explanation for the mysterious communication issues I noticed between people who thought they were speaking the same language, specifically between prisoners and prison ministry volunteers.[6] My professor had never heard of MGT, and asked me about it. In formulating an answer, I realized something meaningful and useful about MGT was being overlooked.

------

[6] For an in depth analysis of MGT, please see my book *Hidden Power & False Expectations: Muted Group Theory for Urban Mission*. Urban Loft Publishing, 2020.

MGT accounts for communicative misunderstandings by looking at relative power between those who are trying to communicate. Please note that the word "muted" here does not mean that persons cannot verbally speak. Instead, MGT uses the term "muted" to refer to persons who have something to say, but are either not allowed to say it or are not heard when they do speak (Ardener 2005). In MGT, those with relatively more power are referred to as the dominant, and those with relatively less power are referred to as subdominant. I will, therefore, initially use this language to present and discuss MGT's five basic tenets. There will be later discussion in Chapter 4 of who exactly is the subdominant, who is the dominant, and where we each fit in those categories.

Tenet #1. *The dominant group creates the language of power and policy.* This means that there is always a group that has more say than the rest in any culture or society. Further, this dominant group creates its own way of saying things. Finally, those who are dominant have the privilege to make decisions for both themselves and others.

For example, who wrote the Constitution of the U.S.? The white guys. Who is it, precisely, who makes the laws? It is still disproportionately male and white politicians. The persons who get to make the crucial decisions have enough power to implement and enforce those decisions. Who sits on the Supreme Court and interprets the U.S. Constitution? Again, it is primarily white men and a few others who have learned the language. Who decides what "Standard English" is, and why is it generally considered more acceptable and legitimate than Ebonics? The same people decide what constitutes academic standards and develop standard academic styles such as APA, MLA, and Chicago. These persons also have the resources for obtaining the education and powerful positions by which they perpetuate their policies. Historically in the U.S., it is the white male who holds the most power. But the story does not end here.

Tenet #2. *The differing life experiences of the dominant and subdominant groups result in communications gaps and the muting of the subdominant.* Different people have different life experiences, and different groups of people have relatively more or less power. The further the spread in how much power people have, the more different their experiences are, and the more likely that the dominant group's language (those with more power) does not adequately describe the life of the subdominant group (those with less power).

A communication gap occurs when a subdominant group member cannot find a word to adequately express something that is outside the dominant group experience. For example, how does a woman explain pregnancy and childbirth to a man? Or, what does the word "hungry" mean to a rich person? Again, what does "convicted of sin" mean to a prisoner? Even if the subdominant group creates words to describe their experience, how does subdominant make the dominant group understand, or just as important, decide to care? The experiences of the other group, the subdominant, are often simply considered irrelevant. Even if the subdominant group develops or revises a vocabulary to adequately describe their life experiences, the dominant group does not perceive any need to accept or learn that vocabulary.

And that results in muting.

Muting occurs when a person's voice is not heard, not recognized, or not respected. Muting is like pressing the "mute" button on the TV; there is something intended to be heard, but no one is paying attention. Or muting is like a large Zoom meeting when the host mutes all other participants to keep them from interfering with the primary speaker. During the COVID 19 pandemic, we held church services on Zoom. And while our music director was broadcasted playing hymns on his piano, the rest of the congregation members were at home singing our hearts out. But no one heard us. I could see the mouths moving on the tiny thumbnails of my church family, but I could not hear their voices. There were technical reasons that such muting was appropriate during those Zoom meetings. But imagine a world where some persons are never unmuted. Unfortunately, for too many subdominant people, this is their reality.

Sermonette: MGT and God's Attitude About Muting

Psalms tells us that we do not have a God who mutes us, but rather a God who hears our voices. Psalms 10:17 says, "O Lord, you will hear the desire of the meek; you will strengthen their heart, you will incline your ear." Again, in Psalms 17:6, "I call upon you, for you will answer me, O God; incline your ear to me, hear my words." And yet again, "I waited patiently for the Lord; he inclined to me and heard my cry."

Jesus is an amazing example of someone who refrained from muting others. When the blind men were calling out to Jesus and the crowd ordered them to be quiet, Jesus listened to them and took pity on them (Matt. 20:30-34). In Luke 4:7-30, 39, Jesus talked with, and listened to, the outcast Samaritan woman. Further, he gave her a new vocabulary, that of living water, with which she was able to communicate to her village. Another example occurs in Matthew 15:21-28, when Jesus meets a Canaanite woman. Jesus did not initially answer her, and went so far as to try to silence her at the request of his disciples. But when she refused to be silenced, Jesus not only listened, but he commended her faith and healed her child. Finally, we are given an account of Jesus literally healing a deaf man with speech impediment, causing "the mute to speak" (Mark 7:31-37).

These scriptures are examples that show God's attitude toward silencing others. If we want to follow his example, we will instead listen to the voices of the less powerful and the oppressed. Scripture lays it out clearly: we are told to "Open your mouth for the mute, for the rights of all the unfortunate" (Prov. 31:8).

Tenet #3. *The subdominant group either must learn and use the language of the dominant, or suffer the loss of societal benefits.* Since the powerful control language, those with less power are at a disadvantage. So, while the dominant group does not need to learn the vocabulary of the subdominant, there is a price to pay the other way around if the subdominant does not learn the dominant language. As a professor, I am required by the institution that hired me not to pass students who cannot write in standard English. I expect my students to submit papers written in "standard English" and follow a prescribed style, such as MLA. Thus, while I attempt to assist students in learning how to write "acceptable" papers, I am very aware of the irony that I am acting as a muter.

I have heard people of my generation who do not like, appreciate, or tolerate rap music. This is simply another example of the dominant (older, mostly white, professional) group who does not value the language created by subdominant group members (younger, often non-white, less affluent) to describe life experiences that the dominant group does not understand. The language and message of rap reflect real shared experiences and attempt to communicate important and relative truths. However, most of that communication remains intra-group since the dominant society often simply tunes it out.

Prison has its own languages. I use the plural here intentionally. There is the language that is created by those in power, the official language. There also exists the language of the less powerful, of the prisoners.

In California, official prison language is mandated by the Department of Corrections and Rehabilitation in Title 15 of the California Penal Code. Section 3000 alone begins with a list of 248 definitions of terms. A brief sample includes:

Central File (C-File) means a master file maintained by the department containing records regarding each person committed to its jurisdiction.

Criminogenic Need means an attribute of the inmate that is directly linked to criminal behavior.

Ex-Offender means a person previously convicted of a felony in California or any other state, or convicted of an offense in another state which would have been a felony if committed in California.

Indigent Inmate means an inmate who has maintained an inmate trust account with twenty-five dollars ($25) or less for 30 consecutive days.

Inmate means a person under the jurisdiction of the Secretary and not paroled. Inmate and prisoner are synonymous terms.

Prisoner means a person in custody of the Secretary and not paroled. Prisoner and inmate are synonymous terms.

Program failure means any inmate who generates a significant disciplinary history within the last 180 days from the current date. A guilty finding for two serious Rules Violation Reports or one serious and two administrative Rules Violation Reports within that 180 day time period is reasonable evidence of a significant disciplinary history and may be considered a program failure.

Rehabilitative Programs are programs managed by the Division of Rehabilitative Programs (DRP), to equip inmates with career opportunities, and to assist them in dealing effectively with the challenges of life, in preparation for successful reintegration into the community.

Created by those in power, all prisoners need to learn this first language in order to respond correctly, stay out of trouble, or be aware of their rights. I learned this language particularly well when, for some years, I worked as an "incident clerk," typing up the reports officers were mandated to write about any event considered an incident (such as a fight). Since these were legal documents that could eventually be used in court to convict or acquit someone of an additional crime, accuracy was crucial. I was able to turn this knowledge to my advantage when it came time to make any sort of formal written complaint using the departmental appeal form (CDCR form 602). Most of the 602s I wrote, both for myself and others, were granted.

However, the second language, the language of prisoners, is filled with new terms that describe the unique carceral experiences of prisoners, as well as with old words that have gained new shared meanings. For the appeal process described above, "to 602" is now a verb: "I'm going to 602 my disciplinary write-up." To "blue slip" means to send an official "Inmate Request for Interview" form to staff, whether to ask for indigent supplies, a visiting form, or any other need. I actually remember when, in the early 1980s, these forms were printed on blue paper. Most people currently incarcerated do not. We have "bunkies" or "cellies," not roommates. It is not just resistance to the term because we live in cells and not rooms. "Cell mate" usually implies a less personal relationship with someone who just moved into your cell. But "bunkies" form special bonds, become intimate in ways beyond explanation from sharing a 7x9-foot cell all day and all night, and from the shared joys and traumas of prison.

Tenet #4. *Resistance and change are possible.* If the dynamics of muting cannot be changed, then MGT is useless, simply describing the *status quo* but giving no hope. However, MGT provides reason for optimism!

One example is the relatively new acceptance by society of the concept of "sexual harassment." In my youth, no one had heard this phrase. Previous to the coining of this term by Pulitzer Prize-winning writer Lin Farley in 1978, the behavior it described was considered "just a part of life" and a problem without a name (Kitzinger & Thomas 1995). The subdominant group, in this case primarily women, were very aware that they were under pressure to accept sexual advances and "play the game," or suffer the consequences of losing their jobs. But slowly, especially as more women gained some degree of power within the marketplace and the courts, the term "sexual harassment" came to have meaning within the dominant culture. With the #MeToo movement in which subdominant group persons find their voices and verbalize their life experiences, "sexual harassment" has become relevant to the dominant culture. It has attained a place in dominant vocabulary.

Another recent movement occurring within many of our churches that shows how resistance and change can look is contemporary worship services. Fifty years ago, most churches sang hymns from traditional hymnals. But with the advent of rock and roll, a new style of Christian music emerged that was more relevant and spoke to the life experiences of the youth. Initially, some churches thought rock and roll was the music of the devil and totally rejected it. Then churches began to see this new music as a language of the young, and a way to reach out to those who did not relate to traditional church music. Gradually, many churches have come to recognize that Christian worship incorporating both heart-language (ways of speaking that are closest to someone's heart) and culturally appropriate music is valid and should be respected. Contemporary worship music has thus entered the repertoire of many churches.

Tenet #5. *These dynamics occur even between groups with a micro power differential.* By micro power differentials, I refer to groups who are close but not identical in power. Prior to my research, MGT was mainly used to describe gendered communication. The dominant group was men, the subdominant group was women, and the difference in power was large and obvious. A few academics used MGT to describe communication between black and white Americans. In both cases, the distance between the two groups in terms of power was considered both great and fixed. No one moved from one group to the other.[7]

My work has consisted of reevaluating the relative power distance between dominant and subdominant groups. I have proved that the same MGT power dynamics are at work between groups with micro power differentials, where the relative power is much closer. These small power differentials are much more likely to be overlooked, especially in the face of obvious macro power differentials such as gender and race. Most people easily grasp that the power differential between prisoner and guard are huge and fixed. It is rather obvious that within the prison, the incarcerated person is subdominant to any and all staff, and that there is no going back and forth between the two groups. However, my research showed that MGT power dynamics was just as applicable to the communication between women prisoners and women prison ministry volunteers as it was between white men and everyone else, making it clear that the categories are not fixed (Kramarae 2005).[8] The specific findings of my research, which are especially relevant to prison ministry, are something that I will discuss at length and in detail in detail in Chapters 5 and 6. But first, the following is an example of how small power differences can be at work in an everyday situation.

---

[7] Those who did attempt to move from one of these groups to another, in particular transsexual individuals, or those who had light skin and could thus "pass" for white, were historically held suspect if discovered.

[8] Cheris Kramarae, who brought MGT from obscurity as a theory in anthropology to the world of gendered communication, has remarked, "What a wonderful contribution to the theory, making clear that the categories are not fixed." (Cheris Kramarae, personal correspondence, 2019).

I had only been out of prison for two weeks when Megan, a dear friend, supporter, and benefactor during my years of incarceration, picked me up from the halfway house where I was living in order to treat me to a "spa day." It was a lovely gesture. But at one point during our pedicures, I found myself becoming terribly uncomfortable. Megan, as well as her mother and sister, had been customers of this one particular pedicurist, Susie, for many years, and Megan kept insisting to me, "Susie is like family! We just love her, and she knows all about us. And she thinks of us as family too." At this point, Megan addressed Susie directly, "Don't you think of us like family?

Here we were, Megan and I, sitting next to each other in huge, elevated, overstuffed throne-like chairs. Susie the pedicurist was perched on a small stool in front of and below me, hunched over my feet, painting my toe nails. Pedicures were her livelihood. She looked up with a big smile, "Of course I do!"

I was not convinced in the least. And I was horrified that Megan had no clue about the power difference between her and Susie. It is true that all three of us were white women and that we all spoke English. However, we were not all speaking the same language. It was apparent to me that Megan had the power and resources, being a regular paying customer, and Susie had much to lose by disagreeing with her.

As someone newly released from prison, I identified much more closely with Susie at that moment than I did with Megan. I was as unable to confront Megan as Susie was. Megan had written letters to the governor in support of my release. And Megan was paying for this spa day. I was very aware that Megan had more power than I did. And as Susie's customer, I had more power than Susie did. These are the kinds of micro power differentials and communication gaps that MGT explains.

But we will now look at how micro power differences are significant in the greater realm of communication. The reason that this fifth tenet is vital is that within it lies the mechanism for change. Tenet #4, resistance and believing in change, is a prerequisite, but without a reliable mechanism for change, change will not likely occur.

Change never comes easily. I had a sense that what was necessary to bring a dominant group person to resist muting others was compassion, an understanding that the other had been wronged and been caused pain. However, compassion is difficult to attain without some level of commonality of experience. I had been asked to speak at a couple of venues where I would be presenting MGT to a mostly dominant group (white American male) audience. How could I find an example that they could relate to? I needed to find a situation in which they had been subdominant, something that was possible now that micro-level power differences were proven to still result in MGT dynamics with the muting of the subdominant. There are subgroups within the category of "white males" of varying power levels. By tapping into these situations, I could make the concept of muting "relevant" to those formerly always considered to be dominant group members. Absolutely every adult has experienced being a less dominant adolescent. So, by making the concept of muting relevant, compassion for the muted was possible. And where compassion exists, the motivation to resist and change can be developed.

Discussion Questions

1. Are you aware of times when you have been muted? If so, describe what happened. How did this experience make you feel? What societal benefits did you forfeit?

2. Do you believe you are more usually a dominant group member or a subdominant group member? Why? How could this affect your ability to do prison ministry?

3. Have you ever experienced, or been accused of "Mansplaining"? How could this be a type of muting?

4. What areas can you think of outside of prison ministry where muting is an issue?

5. In the example given in this chapter, what do you think Megan and Susie's definitions were for the phrase "like family"? How were they likely similar and/or different? What would your definition of "like family" be in this context?

Chapter 4

Power Dyad Theory – Power Dynamics and Prison Ministry Volunteers

In this chapter, I will talk about how Muted Group Theory (MGT) and power dynamics specifically relate to prison ministry and to ourselves individually. Broad understandings of theory are necessary as groundwork. However, the personal application of theory is what is most important. In Power Dyad Theory (PDT), we will examine the interactions between the nine resulting possible combinations and the nine possible power dyads. But before we do that, we need to look deeper into the underlying power issues of muting.

Muting is in no one's best interest!

Muting is dehumanizing and painful to the one whose voice is not heard. Additionally, muting is counterproductive to open communication. In the short term, muting may seem an effective way to exert power and control over others (think army sergeant barking out orders to new military recruits). However, there are two reasons that muting is not the most effective mode of communication. On the one hand, muting is oppressive and does not result in active cooperation. Quite the opposite, those who are muted may well eventually find the oppression intolerable and revolt. On the other hand, and most importantly for the purposes of this book, muting is not an effective or loving way to minister the Gospel of Christ. It is certainly not how Jesus communicated the gospel message. He listened to the voices of the lowly and outcast, to those such as the woman at the well, blind beggars at the side of the road, and untouchable lepers.

Dominant group members must "own" their power. This is especially true for those doing prison ministry. What we learn in racial reconciliation training applies equally here; some people are simply born into the dominant power group due to no fault of their own. Feeling guilty and pretending that uneven power dynamics do not exist is **not** effective in countering the inequality. Power must be acknowledged before it can possibly be put to effective and moral use.

One of the most surprising results of my doctoral research was in learning that more than half of the prison ministry volunteers that I interviewed were uncomfortable with having more power than the prisoners they were ministering to. Some actually denied that they had power. "No, I don't have more power than they do, unless you mean the part where I have keys and can leave the prison when I want." Others seemed confused by the whole issue of power, referring to Galatians 3:28, "There is no longer Jew or Greek, there is no longer slave or free, there is no longer male and female; for all of you are one in Christ Jesus," as a reason to deny their power difference compared to prisoners.

Nevertheless, volunteers **are** imbued with very real power, power that the prisoner is aware of every minute of every day. This power became even more obvious to me as I was writing in the early days of the coronavirus shelter-in-place lockdown. I heard people repeatedly saying that being told to stop nonessential movement feels like being in jail. I understand that they are not able to go where they want to go. However, in 2009 I endured a six-week prison quarantine lockdown for norovirus, a non-lethal gastro-enteric virus. The difference between the two are remarkable. While sheltering-in-place, I still have unlimited access to showers, I can step into my backyard for fresh air whenever I please, and I have unlimited distance contact with loved ones through phone and Internet. I am still able to choose what food I will eat, and when resources are low, I can choose to take a trip to the grocery store. Finally, and most amazingly to me, on a hot day I can go to my refrigerator for an ice cube! All of this is incredible power that I did not experience in prison. In other words, even if you are *feeling* relatively powerless, you are most certainly more powerful than the most powerful of prisoners.

A prisoner also knows that a simple misunderstanding by a volunteer can spiral out of control and be turned into a major incident. Along with power comes credibility with others in power. Thus, whenever there is an incident, it is the volunteer whose word will stand and the prisoner who is the biggest loser.

How is it that the prisoner or former prisoner is so vulnerable and powerless, even in what seems like innocuous dealings with ministry volunteers? I cannot stress enough how effective the prison structure is in stripping prisoners of power. This is absolutely intentional; stripping people of power makes them easier to control. Shackles and iron bars and uniforms are highly visible reminders of the prisoner's powerlessness. Less visible, but no less impactful, is that prisoners are reduced to an institutional number and/or last name only. This depersonalization erodes a person's identity, especially when contrasted with rules that custody staff must be respectfully addressed by their title, that re-enforces their powerful positions.

Further, consequences for a prisoner for not acknowledging and acceding to the imposed power structure are severe. For shorter term prisoners with determinate sentences, disciplinary "write-ups" can result in loss of good time credits, another way of saying that the prison sentence is prolonged. For life term prisoners with indeterminant sentences, disciplinary "write-ups" are even more devastating, sometimes adding years to a sentence. Prisoners who are not easily controlled are often placed either in higher security institutions or in punishment facilities within the institutions. As a religious volunteer coming into a facility from the outside, you are unlikely to be granted access to these "troublesome" prisoners. The people you will be ministering to are precisely those who are more receptive to abiding by the power structure, and who are most likely to be affected by the inappropriate use of that power against them.

Contrary to possible expectations, this power dynamic does not disappear when a prisoner leaves prison. For one thing, many people leaving prison or jail are then placed on parole, with considerable rules and restrictions upon their behavior. Any infraction of these rules or restrictions may result in re-incarceration. I remember my own surprise in coming to the awareness that being released to a "half-way house" really meant that I was still "half-way" in prison.

The inequality of power continues at least until all constraints are removed. In my case, I was on parole for four years. During those four years, in a particularly painful failing of justice, I was not allowed physical contact with minor children (because the victim in my case was my daughter who I had failed to protect). If I was at a birthday party and someone arrived with a child in tow, I had to immediately leave. Any misunderstand that might cause me to be reported to my parole agent could cause me to be returned to prison for an indefinite time, perhaps years. I never perceived myself to be the most powerful person in a power dynamic.

We also must consider the unfortunate reality of the racial, ethnic, and socio-economic components of the U.S. that result in much higher rates of incarceration for those on the low end of the power spectrum. Poor and minority persons, who are already part of a culture that is primarily subdominant to rich white culture, are far more likely to be convicted of crimes and sent to prison where their power and voice is even more limited. When released from incarceration, these persons generally return to their subdominant culture. This is why I resist using the terms "rehabilitation," "re-integration," and "re-entry." There is no "re" where there was never habilitation, integration, or belonging to the majority culture in the first place.

Please note one more vitally important matter for those looking to do prison ministry, a matter that is equally important for urban ministry (or any ministry, for that matter) to grasp. The fact is that, simply by being the person who is present to instruct and minister the love of Christ, you are imbued with relative power. I have talked with ministry volunteers who understand that there is the power of the Holy Spirit present in such encounters, but are reticent to acknowledge personal power. However, when Paul says "we are ambassadors for Christ" (2 Cor 5:20), to the prisoner this means that, "You are God's representative to me." This is power. The very real presence of the Holy Spirit does not diminish how much personal power is also involved in ministry dynamics.

Power Sharing

What does "power sharing" mean, and how do we accomplish such a thing? I have established that it does not work to simply deny that you have personal power, especially when you are ministering to those who are involved with the criminal justice system. Your power exists whether or not you recognize it or admit it. Moreover, prisoners are aware of your power, also whether or not you recognize it or admit it. Therefore, I ask you to consider an alternative approach to handling your personal power. Instead of trying to equalize the situation by refusing the power that is yours, find a way to use your power to empower the other. If you happen to have power due to race, economic level, education, or other status, this is not a sign of favor from God that allows you to keep the benefits to yourself. We are told that "some would be apostles, some prophets, some evangelists, some pastors and teachers," (Eph, 4:11) which are all positions of power, for a very specific reason. We are "to equip the saints for the work of ministry, for building up the body of Christ, until all of us come to the unity of the faith" (Eph 4:12-13). In other words, any power or privilege we find ourselves imbued with is something that God means for us to use for the benefit of his church. A most particularly effective and moral use of this power is to share that power.

The most obvious way a Christian minister can share power is to bring a deeper understanding of the Gospel message and provide biblical education. Knowledge is power. However, if the prisoner is always only the student, power dynamics remain unchanged. One way to share power entails encouraging and empowering prisoners to grow and ultimately to also teach. An additional benefit to this approach is that it is not only empowering, but you may be amazed at how much the incarcerated have to teach you.

Other ways of sharing power include advocating, lending your voice, power, and credibility to the causes of those who are powerless and voiceless. This could include being an ally in peaceful demonstrations for racial equity, or simply being more informed when you vote and using that power for the benefit of the less powerful.

However, none of us are *always* the most powerful person in all our relationships. And this reality leads us to our next topic where we will focus on communication dynamics at their basic level to see how power sharing can be enhanced.

Power Dyad Theory

Power Dyad Theory (PDT) explores communication dynamics between more and less powerful persons. While the last chapter's discussion of Muted Group Theory (MGT) used the terms dominant and subdominant to refer to group members, in PDT we will be applying these same terms to individuals. We will be looking at communication at its most fundamental level, in the dynamics between two persons, where one is more dominant and the other is subdominant. To do this, first we will sort dominant and subdominant communicators into communication style categories. Only when we have done so can we then use PDT to examine the power dynamic present in each of the nine resulting communication dyads.

These discrete categories of communicators are based on awareness and intent: awareness is a prerequisite. Until a dominant group member is aware that muting exists as an issue, there can be no intent to resist or engage in muting. However, once the person with more power is aware of muting and its dynamics, unless there is active resistance to the muting of others, muting will occur and must be considered intentional. I know this sounds like harsh judgment, but imagine how much harsher it feels to the less powerful person who is muted.

Awareness is not an issue in the same manner for subdominant group members. This is because those who are muted are almost certainly aware of it. The less powerful person might not be knowledgeable regarding the specific dynamics of muting, and may even overlook some incidents of muting. However, unlike Zoom meeting muting where speakers may be oblivious that their microphone is muted until listeners begin tugging on their ears and sending chat messages to unmute, in face-to-face communication the muted are aware that the issue exists. Specific communication gaps might not be identifiable; I might not know *which* of my words are meaningless to you, but I am certainly aware that you are not hearing what I am trying to say!

Categories of Subdominant Communication Styles: How do people react to being muted? One group of scholars described three categories of subdominant communicators specifically based on reactions to muting (Meares et al 2004). Their excellent work was focused on workplace communication, where power structures are generally well defined. Since I find their categories useful, I will be using their category labels here. My own research into micro-level power dynamics has affirmed that their categories are valid even where power structures are less well-defined. Please keep in mind that the same person may, at different times and especially with different communication partners, react in ways consistent with each of these categories.

Muted but Engaged (E): The muted but engaged subdominant group member experiences muting but continues to attempt to communicate. Using the language of Muted Group Theory (MGT), remaining engaged with the communication partner(s) allows the muted communicator both to (a) learn the language of the dominant in order to reap societal benefits, and to (b) resist and possibly change the dominant society. Muted but engaged persons remain constructive and have not given up trying to work through the system, despite frustrations from either not being heard and/or not receiving a respectful response from the dominant group.

Angrily Disengaged (D): The angrily disengaged person experiences muting but, due to frustrated efforts, no longer attempts to continue effective communication. Experiencing a limited agency, angrily disengaged persons project anger in order to avoid the situation and/or avoid interacting with the dominant group communicator.

Resigned and Apathetic (W): The resigned response is the far end of the disengagement continuum. It is an extension of angrily disengaged, but where there no longer remains any optimism that change is possible. The muted persons therefore respond by becoming resigned and apathetic. This ultimate reaction to muting is to withdraw physically and emotionally. The issue that a resigned and apathetic response presents is that there can be no change if the muted conversation partner has withdrawn and left the conversation.

Categories of Dominant Communication Styles: In response to the above categorizes, I have identified three parallel categories of dominant persons, also based on reactions to muting. Again, it is possible that the same person may, at different times and especially with different communication partners, react in ways consistent with each of these categories.

Active and Respectful Learner (R): This category describes the dominant group member who is 1) aware of the existence of power dynamics in communication, 2) believes that subdominant group members may have valuable contributions to offer, and 3) is willing to make an effort to refrain from muting others.

Oblivious and/or In Denial (O): As the name states, these dominant group members are either 1) unaware of muting and power dynamics, and/or 2) are in denial as a defense mechanism so that they do not have to confront power dynamics. This is the only category of communicator that is, in fact, truly unaware of power dynamics.

Knowing and Intentional Muter (I): These are dominant group persons who are not only aware of their power, but use that power to maintain control, often by muting others. The intention to mute may not be an intention to harm. For example, the ultimate intent of the drill sergeant in silencing recruits is to train soldiers and save lives. Nevertheless, the intentional muting of others is not without repercussions.

The Nine Power Dyads

Power dyads are groups of two persons, where the two people are not equal in power. Now that we have labels for these categories of communicators, we can examine what happens when people from different categories interact with others. We will look at each of the nine possible permutations of power dyad configurations. For each of these power dyads, I will describe the defining power dynamic as well as suggest mechanisms and techniques that can be employed to sustain or improve communication within that dyad. I will also evaluate the effectiveness of that dyad for communication purposes, discussing to what varying degree communication within each dyad is either effective, ineffective, or toxic.

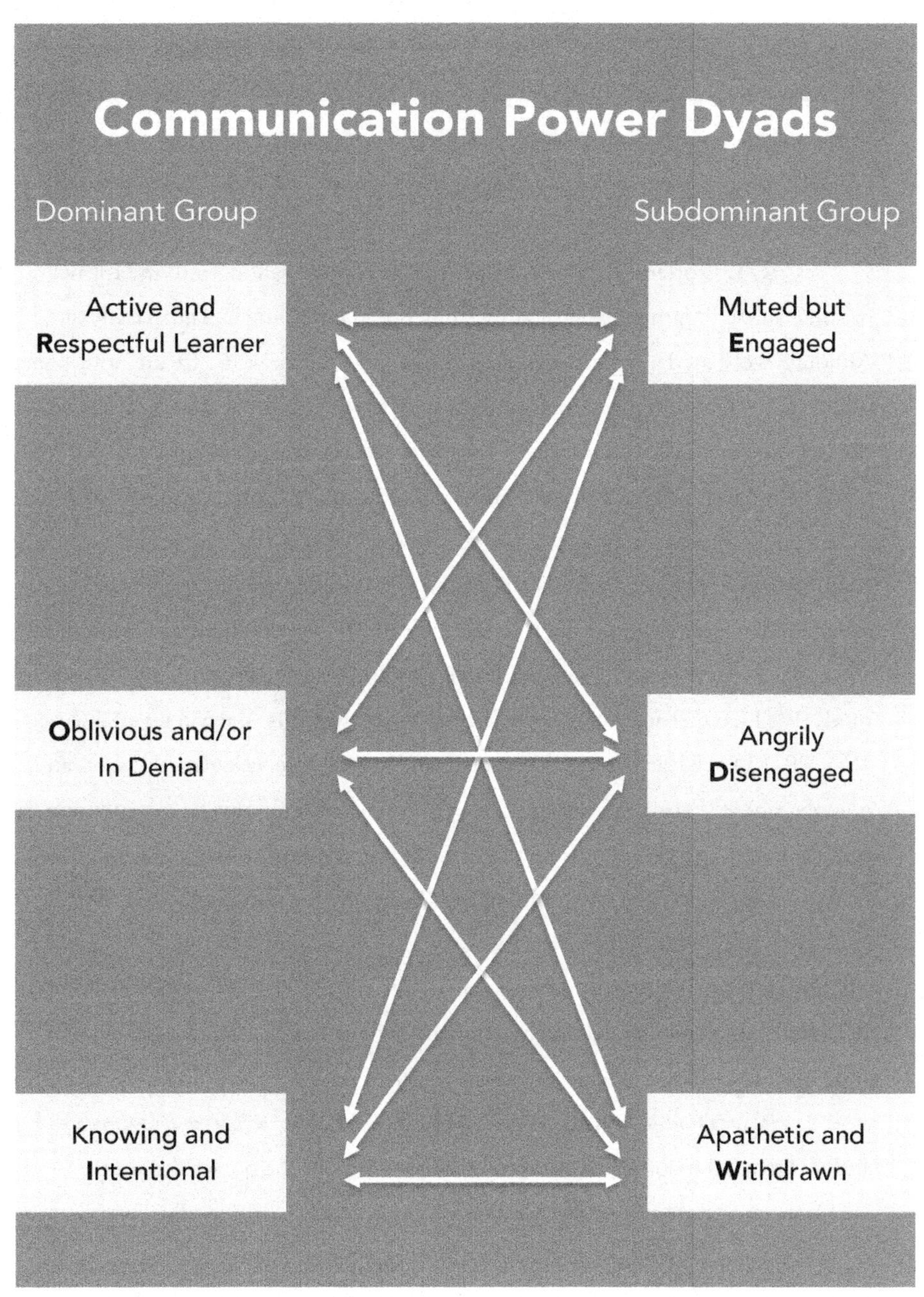

Power Dyad #1 - R/E (Active and Respectful Learner with Muted but Engaged):

The **R/E** dyad is the optimal pairing in Power Dyad Theory. In this most effective dyad, both parties are invested in creating and maintaining a productive and mutually respectful communication encounter. Communication gaps still occur, but there is bilateral awareness of the very real possibility of honest miscommunication. Good communication skills such as active listening and mirroring, restating what the listener thinks was said and asking for clarification, are particularly effective skills for both dominant and subdominant communicators to practice.

R/E is often the power dynamic of my conversations with my former prison cellmate, Martina, when I am visiting her in her home in Tijuana, Mexico. Although we shared a tiny prison cell together for thirteen years, we are not of equal power, and we both know this. From her perspective, I am the educated and very rich white woman who emotionally, spiritually, and financially supports her. On one hand, although I have earned much trust, she still worries greatly about saying things that might displease me and cause me to withdraw even a fraction of this support. If I only listen to what her words would mean in a standard English conversation, I miss much of what she is trying to communicate. To the uninitiated, it might even seem as if Martina tells me outright lies. For example, if I ask her directly whether the funds that I have brought her are sufficient to pay her bills, she will invariably say "Yes." But I have learned to ask what each of her bills are, calculate the sum, and note that there is none left over for groceries! When I bring this to her attention, her eyes invariably sparkle with delight because I have understood her. She will then admit that she didn't want to "burden me" by asking for too much, but that she does in fact need a few more pesos for food. On the other hand, Martina is my teacher who explains her culture and advises me how to avoid being misunderstood. In the grocery store I teach her how to comparison shop, but she teaches me how to appropriately behave and speak while shopping.

Power Dyad #2 - R/D (Active and Respectful Learner with Angrily Disengaged): In an **R/D** dyad, the dominant group member is aware of the power dynamic. However, the subdominant **D** member has experienced a degree of muting that results in anger, frustration, and a refusal to engage. The dominant person has an opportunity to transform an otherwise toxic encounter by using active listening skills to attempt to defuse anger and thereby encourage change. Challenging the **D**'s anger is not likely to be beneficial. However, asking pertinent questions, showing interest in and listening to the answers provided, and validating the subdominant **D**'s experiences of previous muting are possible avenues to eliciting engagement and promoting effective communication.

While still in prison, and later upon parole, I worked as a tutor for Chaffey Community College.[9] Especially in prison, many of the students I was working with had frequently experienced muting. For these students, it was very threatening for me to go over their written papers with them. Some were only present because their professors had made tutoring a condition of them passing the class they were taking. Any criticism or correction of their work was likely to elicit an angry response and a threat to leave the session. I learned to take time to listen, and to not take their anger personally. "Please, help me to understand what you meant. You have very good thoughts and ideas. So, let's figure out how you can help your professor understand how smart you are and what good ideas you have." This approach was not universally successful, but it sometimes made a radical difference in the communication dynamic with an otherwise angrily disengaged student.

Power Dyad #3 – R/W (Active and Respectful Learner with Apathetic and Withdrawn): Again, in this dyad the dominant **R** group member is aware of the power dynamic. However, communication is not effective due to the non-participation of the subdominant **W** member. For the dominant **R** communicator to use active listening skills is not enough to promote effective communication, since the subdominant W has withdrawn and is not attempting to communicate. Additional action from the **R,** including actively inviting and enticing the **W** to participate in the conversation, is necessary in order to develop effective communication. The wider the spread of power difference between the two, the more difficult the gap is to overcome. However, if the **R** is able to span the gap, the more powerful the **R** is perceived to be, the more profound the experience of being heard will be for the **W**.

How communication dynamics can change was brought home to me dramatically at a local mission, a men's shelter, where Sunday late afternoon services

------

[9] Chaffey Community College, in 2005, was the first California community college to re-instate associate degree programs in prisons in the twenty-first century. I worked for them as an "Inmate Facilitator/Tutor" from the inception of this program until I paroled in 2010, at which time I was hired as a tutor for the Chaffey College main campus.

are followed by a community meal. My church was providing both the service and the meal on this particular Sunday, and I had been asked to bring my guitar and lead in a few worship songs. Afterwards, my husband and I were invited to join the attendees at their meal. We sat at the bench table, in the middle and surrounded by homeless men, and tried to initiate conversation. The food, while important, was not so delicious as to account for how much attention it was paid. The men answered our questions with a few monosyllabic responses. The coordinator walked by and tried to fix the situation. "Hey you guys, this lady is from our church! This is Doctor Barkman!" No one looked up.

I laughed and said, "Being a doctor is not why I am here. I served thirty years as a prisoner at the California Institution for Women over in Chino!" Heads lifted, eyes lit up, and the chatter began.

"Hey, I only did twenty years at CIM! You've got me beat!" one man cackled.

"I just got out of jail yesterday," another explained.

And the stories began to flow, one by one, while we interacted. Certainly, the fact that we had something in common made a difference. But these men were not going to risk even attempting to communicate to a dominant PhD, when experience had taught them that they would most likely just be muted instead of understood. But giving them a reason to believe that I would be interested in their stories, that I would hear them, opened communication flood gates.

Power Dyad #4 – O/E (Oblivious or In Denial with Muted but Engaged): In this dyad, the dominant **O** dyad member is not consciously aware of using power in a way that mutes the subdominant. However, the subdominant **E** dyad member is not only aware of being muted, but is actively trying to exercise voice in order to be heard. This dyad is one that is usually ineffective as it forces the subdominant **E** into an uphill battle to overcome the inertia of the dominant **O** person. However, it is easier to change obliviousness than it is to change the aggression of an entrenched defense mechanism such as denial. It is possible for the subdominant **E** to counter cluelessness by engaging and informing the **O** dyad partner, "Did you know that there are people in the room who are not actively participating because they think you won't really listen to them? They are intimidated by your position as a freeperson volunteer." However, this approach is unlikely to work against entrenched denial.

Power Dyad #5 – O/D (Oblivious or In Denial with Angrily Disengaged): In this usually ineffective dyad, neither member is owning their own contribution to the failure to communicate. The oblivious **O** dominant member is unaware of the effect of power dynamics at play, whether in general or within this particular interaction. Due to a history of having been muted in the past, the subdominant **D** member does not perceive that angry responses are any more ineffectual than engaged responses.

Unfortunately, I have seen this dynamic play out during Bible studies in prison. Prisoners, who understand that they are subject to negative consequences if reported for angry outbursts, often express anger by simply walking away in disgust. The dominant **O** member is then likely to attribute any perceived emotion or problem to the subdominant; "I didn't say anything wrong, so why is she angry? She just walked out!" Change within this dyad is unlikely to occur without external stimuli. Although possible, it is unlikely that the anger projected by the **D** member will impose enough discomfort to cause **O** to introspect. Thus, the communication issues are difficult to resolve without the assistance of a mediator. The dominant group member must become willing to self-identify as part of the problem, to introspect, and to take responsibility for improving communication. Additionally, the subdominant **D** can be encouraged to attempt engaging by teaching **D** engagement skills and mechanisms.

Power Dyad #6 – O/W (Oblivious or In Denial with Withdrawn and Apathetic): There is no existing agent for change within this ineffective communication dyad dynamic. With neither the dominant nor the subdominant members able to identify or engage in changing this relatively stable dynamic, status quo can be maintained indefinitely. The **O/W** dyad can be seen in classrooms, where some dominant **O** teachers present educational materials in a "take it or leave it" manner to **W** students who feel powerless to ask questions or otherwise engage with materials and are in a downward spiral of failure. In order to destabilize this dyad, some sort of outside agent is necessary.

For the dominant **O** dyad member, being challenged to ask and answer questions regarding perceptions about, and effectiveness of, communication might begin a positive change in the mindset. These questions might include: (1) Am I getting any feedback that suggests that this person is actually engaging with me? (2) Have I said or done anything that might have prevented a response from this person? (3) Am I hearing anything new from the other person, or am I simply hearing my own words being given back to me? and (4) Is the power differential between us so great that I am accidentally intimidating the other member of my communication dyad?

For the subdominant **W** dyad member, an outside interaction in which the W member actually experiences being heard and validated may encourage the W to attempt engagement. Where the power differential between dominant and subdominant are great, mediation might need to be more active. A mediator's presence can lend power and reduce perceived threat to the subdominant W who has withdrawn due to fear as well as apathy.

Unfortunately, I have observed this dynamic at work between the outside prison ministry volunteers and my sister prisoners at CIW. They say such things as, "Sister Donna is so nice, and I know she loves us. But she just gives us the same salvation message every time. She doesn't understand that some of us have been maturing and growing in the Lord for years and years. And I can't tell her because she doesn't hear me. So, I go to her service, but I don't say anything. As I said, she loves us and I don't want to hurt her feelings. And there isn't really anything I can do about it." Both sides are losing out in this exchange. But even I, as a muted but engaged prisoner, found this particular power dynamic too fraught with danger and potential losses to challenge.

Power Dyad #7 – I/E (Knowing and Intentional Muter with Muted but Engaged): The defining term for this dyad pairing is "power struggle." In this minimally effective and moderately toxic dyad, the subdominant **E** is attempting to engage the dominant **I**, whose intention is to maintain power, not to engage. In order to improve communication and minimize muting, the goal here is to convince the dominant **I** dyad member that muting is not in his or her best interest, that there might be value to the **I** in what the **E** has to offer. The subdominant **E** member will be best served by appealing to the goals and values of the **I**; "I have information that you need."

In my experience, humor can be a powerful weapon in the power struggles inherent in this communication dyad. Direct challenge is likely to deepen the intentional muters sense of power threat, while a soft answer deflects the perception of being challenged while still getting some content across.

Unfortunately, in the example I present here, I was the knowing and intentional muter. In a recent Zoom meeting with several leaders from my church, I reacted in impatience and frustration with someone I felt, at that moment, had not understood a point made at a previous meeting. I initially thought I had politely addressed the situation, and headed off an attempt to take the meeting off course. In other words, I knew what we were supposed to be talking about, and when someone voiced something contrary, I muted him. It was not until a later follow-up email was sent by this person stating, "that's the sort of thing I had in mind when I made an early comment and got quickly cut off in our group on Thursday," that I realized what I had done. I read that, and my heart sank. Here I am, with my PhD in communication theory, writing books about why we should not mute others, and I find myself guilty of doing exactly that to a wonderful, gentle, brilliant retired missionary. But it was the gentleness of this implied rebuke from someone who had been muted but remained engaged that allowed me to see what I had done, and apologize. At the next meeting of the same group, I acknowledged that I had been guilty of silencing our

Not all muting is racist, but racism is always muting.

An ultimate, tragic example of intentional and knowing muting is that which happened to George Floyd in 2020. None of us will quickly forget the image of the Black man lying face down on the ground while a white police officer pressed a knee into his neck. The words "I can't breathe" had no meaning to the white officer, who had no intention of listening. As a result, George Floyd forfeited the ultimate in societal benefits, his very life, in this notorious eight-minute forty-six-second episode. Furthermore, the young girl who videoed the incident was also muted. She was talking, she was asking the police to let George Floyd breathe, but no one was listening. The power divide between an intentionally muting dominant white police officer and a muted but engaged subdominant African American teenaged girl was too great for her to surmount.

brother's voice, and asked forgiveness. I restated the comment that preceded my muting him, and invited him to help us understand his intention.

Power Dyad #8 – I/D (Knowing and Intentional Muter with Angrily Disengaged): The **I/D** is the most toxic of the power dyads, because in this pairing neither side has any intention to value or listen to the other. The subdominant **D** has a need to express the pain of having been muted, and this expression is in the form of anger, defiance, and rage. The dominant **I** has no acknowledged interest in hearing but instead attempts to exert power and silence the subdominant member. This interaction is likely to spiral out of control, especially if the **D** continues to target and discharge anger while disengaging from the actual communication aspect of the interchange. The **I/D** is the underlying communication dynamic of such unfortunate and explosive events as the Los Angeles riots of both 1965 and 1992.

A mediator is usually necessary to resolve the inherent communication gaps between these dyad members. It might be possible (although still difficult) to propose to the subdominant **D** that engaging could be beneficial, especially if the mediator is an Active and **R**espectful Learner who models listening as an alternative to muting. The mediator's best approach to the dominant **I** member would be interest-based negotiation. The difficulty in this approach, presenting the idea that muting is not in the best interest of the **I**, is that the **I** often cites the angry responses of the **D** as proof that muting is justified and needed.

I see this dynamic in some of the less peaceful riotings immediately following the tragic deaths of more of my African American brothers and sisters at the hands of police. For example, in a Facebook discussion of the events following the death of George Floyd, I read responses such as "There is no excuse for looting and violence! I understand that wrongs have possibly happened, but they should protest quietly and without violence." I agree in part; I do not advocate violent reactions. However, dominant U.S. culture must understand the dynamic behind these not-so-peaceful protests. These are often the reactions of the angrily disengaged who feel that their voices are not listened to and that "quiet" protest is a protest that can be ignored. If those in power had been listening to "quiet" voices, they would have heard the multiple voices decrying all along the implicit racism in police responses resulting in Black Americans' death.

Power Dyad #9 – I/W (Knowing and Intentional Muter with Withdrawn and Apathetic): In this unfortunate and toxic pairing, power is so successfully exerted against the subdominant that the dominant group member is in total control of the communication. Power and communication flow are unidirectional. Radical examples of this often-abusive power dyad include military general to private, master to slave, and pimp to prostitute.

In order to improve communication, the dominant **I** must come to value the potential contribution of the subdominant member, which is nearly impossible to accomplish without a mediator speaking on behalf of the **W** member.

A Mechanism for Change

In the original MGT model where dominant generally meant male and white, a designation that was permanent and fixed, the dominant group member functioned permanently in that position of power. However, now that we know that MGT dynamics are at work even when there is only a minimal power difference, we all are sometimes the dominant person in a power dyad. At other times, we all experience being the subdominant communicator. What makes this detail important is that if we have all been subdominant at some time, if we have all been muted at some time, then we can build on that experience to build empathy. And empathy, identifying with what another person is going through, is key in changing behavior. As long as muting is a technique working for a powerful person, especially if that powerful person is always the most powerful person, there is little obvious reason for that person to change. However, if we can identify a time when we were muted and consider how hurtful and ineffective the resulting communication resulted, this provides a reason to consider changing muting behavior.

Thus, even a very successful dominant white male can relate to having been a child who was subdominant to parents, or a student who was subdominant to a professor, and was thereby muted. As an example, I am confident that every adult was at one time a teenager. And teenagers are subdominant to adults. Further, youth always have a culture different from the adults because they work so hard to develop precisely that in their struggles to create a distinct self-identity! Therefore, youth develop their own language and experiences that adults do not, generally, appreciate or respect. "No, you will not play that awful music on the radio in MY car!" the parent exclaims to the disgust of the teenager. The dominant group member can be asked to remember those experiences as that teenager and what it felt like to be muted. Did being muted feel good? Did being muted make you want to cooperate? Did your being muted make the communication better or worse?

We have hopefully realized, by reading these last two chapters on MGT and PDT, that being muted does not feel good. Muting does not create a good communication environment. And muting does not result in positive communication encounters. Therefore, it is in everyone's best interests to learn how to avoid both muting others and being muted.

1. How might MGT power dynamics prove a unique challenge to incarcerated persons who previously experienced the status of being white, powerful, and financially influential?

2. What specific ways could you possibly enact "power-sharing" within your present ministry context?

3. Which power dyad do you most frequently find yourself a member of? Why is that? How effective is communication for you within that dyad?

4. Find a passage in the New Testament where Jesus is muted. What are the dynamics you see here? How does Jesus respond? What was the effect of his response?

5. How might you answer the questions referred to in Dyad #6 on pages 64 & 65?

Chapter 5

Definition of "Church" and Other Communication Gaps

Now that you have a working understanding of how communication is complicated by differing life experiences and communications styles, it is time to address certain specific issues this causes in prison ministry. Muted Group Theory and Power Dyad Theory describe the *how*, but the next step is to examine the *what* of communication gaps. When communication gaps cause what is being said (or left unsaid) to have a different meaning than what is being heard, serious consequences can result. This is true in any context, and especially true when prison ministry volunteers do not realize that prison has its own language, that the same English words have completely different meanings to those inside the prison than to those outside the system.

Church: One small word that often carries a vastly different meaning to those inside prisons than it does to those doing prison ministry is "church." What does the word "church" mean to you? When you say you are "going to church" you likely mean you are getting in your car and driving to a specific building which is where you attend services. Even during the coronavirus shelter at home, I saw Zoom services that began with a processional video starting in the church patio, entering through the narthex, and continuing into the sanctuary while the prelude music was playing. Church in these terms is a place. Also, you are more likely to be thinking small "c" church; church is *your* church where you gather with like-minded people of one denomination. Church in these terms is a specific group of people. Additionally, it is also likely that you distinguish between a formal church service and other types of gatherings such as Bible studies, social functions, committee meetings, and prayer meetings.

I cannot speak for all prisoners, but most of my prison sisters and I had a very different understanding. Since the California Institution for Women (CIW) had one Interfaith Chapel that the various faiths shared, we referred to that location as the chapel. But we did not think of that location as being "the church." Further, we were more in tuned to being part of the big "C" Church than any specific congregation, since our membership was always in flux, and our leadership consisted of volunteers from so many different churches and denominations.

The greatest difference in our understanding of church came from relying on Matthew 18:20, "For where two or three are gathered in my name, I am there among them." Thus, our understanding was that any activity that was centered on Jesus was "church." The way I discovered that this was a significant difference in definitions, one that constituted a major communication gap, was in looking over the transcripts of an interview I had held with a prison ministry volunteer. In answering a question about how often he participated in church inside prison, he responded "I don't know how to answer that. I didn't really attend church in there because I was just leading a Bible study. But the ladies in there call *everything* church!" And I realized that he was absolutely correct. We did call all of it church because we actually considered it all church. Since we understood church to be anywhere that Jesus was present with us, whether it was a formal church service in the chapel, a Bible study or class held in an educational classroom, a special event held in the auditorium, or a prisoner-held prayer session in someone's cell, we considered it all church. I still tend to define "church" that way even though I have come to understand that most people outside prison do not. To them, the term "church" is reserved for formal worship within the sanctuary.

Why does this matter? I have observed a different underlying attitude in many people about "church" that is held in the sanctuary, and other more peripheral activities, an attitude that, to be frank, confused me in my early years of freedom from prison. I could not understand how a Fellowship Committee meeting could be opened and closed without prayer! After being a member of this committee for some months, and feeling a little secure with my relationships with the other members, I asked why we didn't pray. The other members looked at each other and shrugged. "It's not a problem. You can lead us in opening and closing prayer if you want from now on." And I did, only to be thanked later by two of the members for broaching the subject. They had not realized that prayer was missing.

Thus, how you live out your definition of church might affect how those you minister to are perceiving your attitude about Jesus. If you are thinking you are simply leading a study group, but the people who are attending are thinking of it as "church," it changes things. For one thing, power dynamics change. Your position as leader of this group is thus elevated, and your teaching may therefore have more authority than you realize. Further, a physical location that might at other times of even the same day be considered simply a classroom, may be being perceived during your Bible study or class with all the respect and holiness usually reserved, outside of prison or jail, for the church sanctuary. You could be seen as taking "church" lightly if you are less formal in your behavior because the surroundings do not fit your definition of "church."

Good Church

As if the gap between what you think of as "church" and what incarcerated persons think of "church" were not enough to complicate ministry efforts, there is likely also a great difference between what you think of as a "good church" and what those you minister to are thinking of as a "good church." Most of the prison ministry volunteers who I have interviewed stated a belief that love and support were what prisoners needed most from a church outside of prison. However, most prisoners and former prisoners tell me that acceptance is even more important than love and support. My sisters and brothers who have been in prison also tell me that acceptance is not so easy to find in churches outside.

The culture in many of our churches is such that there is an attempt by the members to project an image that everything is fine. People worry that if the other members of the church become aware that they have unresolved issues such as a mental illness, that they will be judged. This came up in a clergy training meeting I attended yesterday regarding trauma in churches. I was told that church members do not always want to admit to trauma since they fear it implies a lack of faith or spiritual maturity. Such is the opposite of church in jail or prison, where everyone knows that **no one** is really alright. Everyone in prison or jail has recognizable issues and problems by the very nature of incarceration, and it is useless to pretend otherwise. Moreover, being able to bring those problems to Jesus is a vital and important part of church! I have heard repeatedly from my prison siblings that, because of this issue, it feels to them as if church outside prison is phony.

What can be done about this? There are several options. First, we must each take a good hard look at our own churches, and determine the strengths and weaknesses of each church. Every church will have some of each. It is not disloyal to acknowledge where a church falls short of the example of Jesus. Step two is to find ways to possibly help our churches grow further into the example of Christ. And step three is to be forthright and honest to those in prison and jail about what expectations they should be forming about churches, especially your church. You may be surprised to find that giving your honest appraisal increases your credibility and actually draws people to your church, especially people who want to be part of a solution instead of part of the problem.

Why does it matter that incarcerated people look at church differently? It matters because many or most incarcerated people are looking to ministry volunteers to provide information that will help in finding a home church. How can you give them relevant answers if you do not understand what they are asking you for?

Bringing Jesus with You

Many people mistakenly believe that ministry and mission are avenues for bringing Jesus where He was not previously present. Be assured, Jesus is always, **always**, already there. And sometimes He is there more intensely than you can imagine. Prisons and jails certainly can present themselves as dark and Godless places. However, just as certainly, the light of Christ shines brightest in the darkest of places. In one of my favorite quotes from a friend of mine from our time together in prison, "I was on a retreat for twenty-seven years." The presence of Jesus was so real to her that she would say, "The God of the universe was visiting me today in my room." I repeat, Jesus is already in prisons.

So, what are prison ministry volunteers bringing to prison and jail if it is not Jesus? You bring knowledge, wisdom, perspective, and most importantly, tangible proof of Jesus' love. This latter cannot be overstated; you are the flesh and bones of love and acceptance. And you are bringing that love and acceptance to persons who have been deemed by society as being unworthy of inclusion. Additionally, you are bringing your personal power, the power to facilitate activities that the prison or jail would not readily allow without you.

My research has shown that when former prisoners describe a good church, it is one that is overwhelmingly accepting, welcoming and non-judgmental, that teaches the gospel, is small and intimate, and provides intense worship opportunities. However, when prison ministry volunteers describe a good church, it is one that overwhelmingly focuses on teaching the gospel, that is accepting, that is small and intimate, and that serves its members.   While there is much overlap in these two definitions, these are **not** the same church.

Expectations

People in prison are in fact forming expectations of what church is likely to be when they parole, and their communication with prison ministry volunteers is not helping them to develop realistic expectations. Of former prisoners that I have questioned about their experiences when attending churches that had been recommended by prison volunteers, they have unanimously reported that the churches did not meet their expectations. On the other hand, eighty percent of the prison ministry volunteers who knew of former prisoners attending their church assured me that it was a positive experience for those persons. Expectations did not withstand reality.

Prior Church Experience: Upon leaving CIW the only thing I was certain about concerning the churches outside was that I did not know what a "good" church was. Every formerly incarcerated sister or brother who I talked about this with agreed. The logic goes like this, "If any church I had attended before prison had been a 'good' church, I would never have ended up in prison in the first place."

One African American brother strongly contested this point with me a few years ago. His argument was that most of the women he ministered to at CIW, especially those of his culture, had grown up in the church and knew the church very well. The point he missed is subtle, but vital. There is a difference between being "in" the church and being "of" the church. This was borne out in my interviews with former prisoners, many of who admitted to having been raised "in" the church, but

Why People Return to Prison

I am amazed at the number of well-meaning people who have told me that "Some people are just more at home in prison and *want* to go back." My pushback to this has to do with recognizing the difference between *wants* and *needs*.

The argument that I am usually given is that, for some prisoners, life in prison is better than they have ever experienced outside. I am also told that people who have served exceedingly long sentences in prison do not have anyone outside and do not know how to negotiate life beyond the prison walls. And I am assured that it is prisoners themselves that have said these things.

I absolutely believe that prisoners have said these words. However, I have a different perspective on what those words were intended to mean. There are many deeper realities about prison that words cannot adequately communicate (think MGT here!) that are simply understood by insiders. Nevertheless, there is an underlying, if unstated, truth that we all recognize. No one would willingly choose the degradation and dehumanization of prison as their optimal lifestyle.

It is quite true that for some prisoners, prison provides a better quality of food, housing, economic opportunity, relationships, and even safety than the community outside prison does. This statement should not be understood to mean that prison has thus provided something desirable. Instead, it is a glaring condemnation of our society that results in a tragic lack of life opportunities for some to get their needs met. True, for some persons it is necessary to meet the basic needs of life through state provided and issued food, medical care, clothing, and housing. But please do not confuse these desperate *needs* with what a human being created in the image of God actually *wants*. Such a misperception is simply one more layer of degradation and dehumanization.

As to the issue of not knowing how to negotiate life outside prison walls after a long incarceration, I can attest to the truth of those words, too. I came out of prison white, educated, and with family support, and the transition was still incredibly difficult. And I was exceptionally lonely for the constant company of my prison sisters, especially my sisters in Christ, who were ever-present on the inside. But I say again that I came out of prison white, educated, and with family support. These assets made it immeasurably easier for me to be accepted in society outside prison than for my homeless sisters and brothers in the local park who do not have my physical, social, and mental resources. For them, food, shelter, and safety are *needs* that prison is legally mandated to meet, but our society is not.

who did not identify themselves as saved or committed to Jesus until after their incarceration. One of my sisters put it this way, that although many African Americans were raised going to church every Sunday, it was not until prison that church became something where "We worship with all our heart" and "We did it for us, not grandma!"

New Convert Expectations: My research showed that volunteers have realistic expectations of what their churches are offering paroling women, and they believe that they are successful at communicating this to new converts inside prison. Formerly incarcerated persons tell me that realistic expectations are not being communicated to new converts in prison, and that therefore the new converts have unrealistic expectations of the outside churches. And these unrealistic expectations impact these new converts when they are ultimately confronted with reality upon parole. The dynamics of this communication gap lead to a secondary gap that will be further discussed next under the topic of "honesty."

Honesty: Incarcerated people are hoping for a reality check on what the church out there is and what it actually offers. When they do not receive this, it can feel like a lack of honesty from the prison ministry volunteers. I have heard former prisoners voice this as, "Why do they lie to us? Why don't they tell us that they don't have all these resources?"

One prison ministry volunteer I interviewed was amazed that prisoners had taken to heart her assurances that they were able to pass her class, but did so without having understood the unstated requirements that they would have to actually attend class and do the assigned work. "But you promised us we could pass!" The instructor had not understood that the powerlessness of extreme poverty does not equate effort with success; that is a privileged understanding of how structures work.

On the other hand, when I wrote to my friend Cindy who is still incarcerated about the difficulties that most former lifer prisoners have in their relationships with their children, I immediately received a letter expressing her gratitude. Cindy had been blaming herself for issues in her relationship with her daughter. However, she found great comfort in my affirming the tragic truth that decades of separation creates distance that is not so easily overcome.

Transforming New Life in Christ: Many prisoners undergo a remarkable transformation as they experience new life in Christ, a transformation that is acknowledged by both prison ministry volunteers and the prisoners. The gap here is not in perception, but in experience. One volunteer explained to me that "I feel like they've experienced transformation in a way that people who have gone to church for most of their lives don't get…they've tasted of that in a way that people who've been life-long Christians haven't."

And on the other hand, prisoners are often at loss of words to express what this transformation feels like. The words may sound eloquent, like the words of my friend who said, "When you find Jesus in the destitute, in the darkness, when there's nothing to distract you, it's just you and Him." However, she followed this by explaining that there are no words in the English language that truly convey her meaning. "All I can use is our mediocre words, is that it gives you a hope that supersedes anything."

Aggression vs. Power: It may be easy to confuse aggression with power. Sometimes what appears to be aggressive behavior is actually the response of someone who is experiencing powerlessness. There is a saying that even a mouse will attack a cat when it is cornered. I have found that some prison ministry volunteers perceive aggression as prisoners exerting their power, when what they are actually observing may well be what I referred to in Chapter 3 about Muted Group Theory (MGT) as the angrily disengaged response of a muted, less powerful group member.

One of my favorite lines comes from a man who was incarcerated in his youth but now is a pastor who leads a prison ministry team. He was talking about his frustrations about power issues and explained, "When your head is inside the lion's mouth, you don't slap the lion!"

Holidays

This is a topic that you need to come at with a great deal of sensitivity. Holidays have different meanings for different people. Life experiences can greatly influence the meaning of a holiday. Presuming that you can bring the same holiday message you just shared in your home church to incarcerated people is often a mistake.

One case in point would be Mother's Day. This is a particularly painful holiday for me since my own incarceration resulted from the death of my two-year-old daughter. At CIW, I was not alone in finding this holiday difficult. Most women there were mothers. Of those, all were separated from their children, and many had experienced losing all parental rights and contacts with their children, which made motherhood an extremely painful topic. Other women had been incarcerated since their youth and spent all their childbearing years incarcerated with no opportunity to be a mother. Looking at Mother's Day from the opposite direction did not necessarily make the day any easier. Even those who had not experienced abuse or neglect at the hands of their own mothers were, nevertheless, experiencing separation from their mothers. Worse, some bear the guilt that resulted from their mother dying alone while the daughter was incarcerated. And all of this pain is then intensified by the knowledge of our own responsibility for being in the situation that resulted in our incarceration, whether or not we were actually guilty of the crime for which we were imprisoned. Please do not simply presume that honoring all mothers is a message of hope, joy, and comfort to incarcerated women.

Sermonette: Mark 3:32-35

There is nothing wrong with honoring your parents or being honored as parents by your children. However, I have found the following Mother's Day message particularly effective at comforting wounded and/or incarcerated women. This sermon is based on Mark 3:32-35:

A crowd was sitting around [Jesus]; and they said to him, "Your mother and your brothers and sisters are outside, asking for you." And he replied, "Who are my mother and my brothers?" And looking at those who sat around him, he said, "Here are my mother and my brothers! Whoever does the will of God is my brother and sister and mother."

In this scripture, Jesus gives us a brand-new perspective on motherhood and Mother's Day. If we are doing God's will, Jesus actually considers us on par with his own mother, the virgin Mary! Now that is something to aspire to. All Jesus asks is that we do the will of God.

And what is the will of God for us? We find scriptures such as; "For it is God's will that by doing right you should silence the ignorance of the foolish" (I Peter 2:15), "Rejoice always, pray without ceasing, give thanks in all circumstances; for this is the will of God in Christ Jesus for you" (1 Thess. 5:16-18), and "For it is God's will that by doing right you should silence the ignorance of the foolish" (1 Peter 2:15). It does not matter that we have failed as mothers in the past or have been failed by our mothers. As believers who love and serve God, Jesus will honor us as his own mother.

Also, if you have never given physical birth to a child, that is not a problem either. We can become spiritual mothers or fathers. Paul sets the example when he tells us, "For though you might have ten thousand guardians in Christ, you do not have many fathers. Indeed, in Christ Jesus I became your father through the gospel" (1 Cor. 4:15). We can become spiritual children of our elders in Christ and spiritual parents of those we introduce to Jesus or raise up in the Word.

At the other end of the spectrum, many incarcerated people make the most of what they can with holidays. When I worked in the prison Mental Health department as a "peer helper" (we could not be called counselors for legal reasons), my co-workers and I were a total amazement to one of the psychologists with whom we worked closely. Dr. Green was trying to be sensitive to us, and wanted to turn the radio off during the Christmas carol "I'll be Home for Christmas." She could only imagine how painful such lyrics were for women serving life term, and in the case of my office mate, life-without-possibility-of-parole. But she was wrong. The bottom line of that song, a promise that "I'll be home for Christmas, if only in my dreams," was a promise that we could realistically make to our families, loved ones, and ourselves. If we could not be their physically, we did have the power to return home in our thoughts, spirits, and dreams. For my co-workers and me, this was of great comfort. However, I'm not sure that Dr. Green ever really believed us.

Other holiday pitfalls include St. Valentine's Day, which until God did a major healing in my heart I referred to as "Rejection Day." Father's Day is loaded with booby-traps. Whether biological fathers were loving, abusive, or absent, incarceration adds separation to the list of issues.

If you are going to effectively minister God's love to people who have been incarcerated, you must realize that different life experiences really do result in communication gaps. And even if you are only ministering to the extended family and friends of those who have been incarcerated, realize that Mother's Day and Father's Day have very different meaning to children separated from their parents by incarceration. And this holds true no matter the age of the (possibly now fully grown) child.

1. What is your definition of what constitutes church? Why might it be important to understand whether those you minister to have a different definition?

2. How does this chapter inform the kind of message you would present on holidays as part of your ministry?

3. Reading levels: asking prisoners to share in reading can be a lovely way to include them in a service. However, it is important to be sensitive to those who do not read well or at all. In addition, prison populations have much higher levels of reading disabilities than outside prison populations. How might you present written materials to an audience with vastly different reading levels?

4. What strategies could you use to help prevent conveying inaccurate information about churches and resources?

5. What does "welcoming" mean to you?

Chapter 6

Listen to Us! What Prisoners SAY That They Need

The previous chapter explored the communication gaps that often occur between those doing prison ministry and the people they minister to, where communication has been misunderstood. This chapter will take this process a step further as we look at where communication has been silenced.

One complaint I have heard repeatedly from my previously incarcerated friends about those who minister to them, both inside and outside the prisons, is that "they don't listen to us." This may occur out of prejudice and fear. After all, many people are afraid of prisoners and former prisoners, and therefore maintain a distance intentionally. There are also those who minister who are so certain that they already understand the situation that they do not realize there is a need to listen. A very few are so wound up in themselves that they never really listen to anyone. But my experience is that most people who minister are actually trying to listen. The issue is that most people who do prison ministry do not realize that what they are hearing is a truly different language, that the words they are hearing have other meanings than they are expecting. It sounds like English, it has mostly the same vocabulary, but the shared experience behind the language of prison is vastly different from the language at large.

When we minister from our own perspectives, rather than the perspective of those we minister to, what we offer is likely to miss the mark. I am reminded of myself, as a child of about six, wanting to do something special for my parents. They generally slept in on Saturday mornings, and I knew that breakfast in bed was something special. My problem was that I was too young to be allowed to use the stove for cooking, and my recipe repertoire was limited. I still remember the strange looks on my parents' faces as I presented them with one of my favorites, bologna and catchup sandwiches on Wonder bread. They tried so hard to be gracious and appreciative of my gift, but this was just not the breakfast of their dreams. My dad got out of it by saying, since he knew this was my very favorite, that he would save it for me to have for lunch. I knew that my parents were not unhappy with me, but I also knew that serving them breakfast in bed did not turn out the way I thought it should. What I did not know was why.

It is understandable that a six-year-old did not get the whole picture. But this story leads me wonder how often our ministry is similarly ineffective. Our efforts are appreciated and the love intended is received, both of which are positive things. We did not entirely fail! Yet, how much more effectively our time, labor, and resources could have been used if we had a deeper understanding of what the others' experiences were and what they really wanted or needed.

The way to determine what others want or need is to ask them. However, we then have to listen to the answer, whether or not that answer falls in line with what we expect or even what we want it to be. As we have learned by looking at Muted Group Theory in Chapter 3, listening is complicated by communication gaps. These gaps occur when the words we hear are familiar, but have been given a different meaning in order to describe new experiences. However, until we realize and acknowledge that we have muted another person, how do we learn what it is *that was not said?* To bridge some of these gaps, we will next look at a few of the specific issues that those who have been incarcerated have voiced to me about those who are wanting to provide ministry to them.

Acceptance

Almost no one disagrees that prison ministry should include both acceptance of those who have been incarcerated and a sharing of the gospel message of Christ Jesus. Almost. I have occasionally crossed paths with Christians who believe that as long as they are presenting the gospel, they do not really have to like or associate with those they are ministering to. I once heard a former missionary speaking about a colleague who was going back to their mission field to visit, "Rachel says that those people are like family to her. They were certainly never family to me.

Sermonette: Healing is a Process!

Can we accept someone who claims to be a Christian, but behaves in ways we do not approve of? We Christians are often quick to judge the sincerity of other Christians by what we see in their walk that doesn't meet our standards of Christian behavior. I found this to be particularly true of newly committed Christians in prison on both sides of the coin, of judging and of being judged.

It is a wonderful and amazing thing when conversion is accompanied by deliverance. I have seen people who, from the moment they invited Jesus to be Lord of their hearts, no longer craved cigarettes, or alcohol, or drugs. For some, all foul language was simply gone. Others had a brand-new outlook on life. But for most, conversion is simply the beginning of many struggles. To give perspective, I equate these persons to physically ill patients.

Imagine with me going to a series of doctors because you have a persistent skin condition, one that is unsightly and embarrassing. It covers your hands and face where everyone can see it. You try all sorts of treatments and ointments, but nothing works. Finally, you go to the Great Physician, a doctor who has never made a misdiagnosis. This doctor tells you that you are critically ill from an insidious cancer, and that the skin condition is only a side effect. What you need is surgery to remove the cancer.

Like any good physician, he leaves it up to you to accept his diagnosis and treatment. He requires your consent before he performs surgery to remove the cancer. The cure is not easy; surgery hurts, and you bleed for a while. But your physician says you are not done yet. You still need to undergo chemotherapy in order to irradicate all the remaining cancer cells. The chemo is terribly difficult; it leaves you sick and weak after each treatment. All your hair falls out. However, gradually over time, your condition improves. You recover from the chemo. Your surgical wound heals and, although the scar doesn't entirely disappear, you get stronger. And now you suddenly realize that your skin condition is fading. Perhaps the condition disappears completely without you even noticing. Perhaps your physician has you apply just a little medicine to make last traces of the skin condition go away.

Often, I find, the things we judge others for are only symptoms of the deep, soul-killing, festering wounds that life in this fallen world imposes on people. But while we worry about curing the symptom, God is dealing with the wounds hidden so deep that we have no idea that they are there. Of course, we need to pray for healing for our brothers and sisters who are not yet walking the way we believe "real Christians" should walk. But we can make an effort to leave judgment to the Great Physician, who incidentally, has never lost a patient who trusted in him.

They were just people I ministered to." I wonder how accepted those people she ministered to really felt.

Usually, both sides are aware that acceptance and support are important. However, the main issue, the greatest difference, is in which side is believed to be most important. In my research, most prison ministry volunteers believed that nothing was more important than sharing the gospel message. But what I hear from my formerly incarcerated friends, and what I experienced myself, was an even deeper need for acceptance. I do not mean that you should accept the criminal behaviors that usually precipitate the incarceration. But prisoners need is ministry volunteers who accept that we are all imperfect, and that my behaviors do not define who I am. I need for you to believe I am created in the *imago Dei*, the image of God, and find me an acceptable human being if I am to then believe the rest of the message that you are trying to communicate.

Acceptance, love, and support are three very closely related terms that do not mean quite the same thing. Again, when asked which of these was the most important for people leaving prison, my former prisoner friends most often chose "acceptance." However, prison ministry volunteers, when asked the same question, usually thought that "love/support" was what the prisoners most needed. It is very difficult for someone who has not experienced the alienation of being convicted of a crime and sent to prison to understand that acceptance might outweigh even the need for support and love.

The Importance of Physical Support

According to the limited literature that exists on the topic, several physical needs are identified as paramount for the success of anyone, male or female, upon leaving prison. These needs include employment and economic stability, secure housing, drug treatment, health care, and desisting from illegal activity. Almost all persons leaving prison need help with basic living needs like food, clothing, and transportation. Most prisoners do not leave prison with suitable clothing for wearing to a job interview. If their driver's licenses have not expired, it is unlikely that they have a car. Public transportation, if available, is expensive for someone without adequate income.

What might be surprising is that believers coming out of prison, when asked what they thought most important for churches to offer to those leaving prison, are more concerned about receiving spiritual support and acceptance than they are about receiving food. While one third of prison ministry volunteers I interviewed rated food as important, none of the former prisoners did. One of my friends explained that food is something that can be easily found. Parole agents and social services provide contact information for local food banks, pantries, and community meals. However, acceptance and spiritual support are vital "because if you're not rooted and grounded, you're not going to make it."

Returning Women have Special Needs

A key deficit that women experience after release from prison is the loss of social connections, whether this is the result of criminal activity, of imprisonment, or of their own deliberate choice. Visiting rooms in men's prisons are crowded with wives and children, while visiting rooms in women's prisons are relatively barren of men. There are certainly many exceptions to the rule, but when a man goes to prison, his children are frequently left to their mother to raise. It is not unusual for her to remain attached to him and move to a location nearby. However, when a woman goes to prison, her children are often placed with her parents or siblings who do not have the resources to travel or relocate. And let us not forget that while most crime occurs in highly populated urban settings, most prisons are located in distant and out-of-the-way rural locations.

Ignoring the obvious special needs of women leaving prison or jail is a perfect invitation for mothers to return to prison quickly, with serious repercussions to the child as well as the mother. Time lost to prison in a parent-child relationship cannot be made up by either.

Power

Prisoners are at the bottom of the power hierarchy. This is a reality, and you must understand what this means. Those who do not have power are vulnerable and are likely to try to hide that vulnerability behind false bravado, having the mindset that telling you directly where I am powerless and vulnerable makes me even more vulnerable.

Volunteers have more power than criminalized people! This bears repeating. Especially in the U.S. where we like to think that everyone is equal, we often find ourselves afraid, embarrassed, or shamed by our power. When we do, the natural response is to ignore our power, hide our power, or throw our power away. But this response is not very helpful for those who need you to use your power on their behalf. Using your power for others has a name: Advocacy.

Just as those who have been incarcerated need you to understand that you have more power than they do, they also need you to cooperate with their personal empowerment. This may take the form of providing resources instead doing things for them; teach them to fish rather than just throwing them a fish when it is convenient for you. More often, what empowerment means is being a support, a safety net, when they are stepping out into new enterprises. This does **not** mean simply taking over. A common complaint that I have heard regarding prison ministry volunteers is that, like over-protective parents, they often do take over. Whether this relates to organizing a religious event within the prison or helping to furnish a first apartment, taking over is not the same as listening.

Vicarious Experiences

For those who are locked away from the rest of the world, contact with the outside world is precious beyond words. As a prison ministry volunteer you can help connect the prisoner with the world beyond the walls. And yet many volunteers are afraid that they will say the wrong thing and cause pain.

Do not be afraid to share life experiences because you don't want to "rub salt into our wounds." If you are ministering as a pen pal, you will find that most prisoners treasure being invited to share in the mundane, everyday aspects of life. I know how much I enjoyed letters from my aunt in Wisconsin, who simply described the details of the changing seasons in her back yard. It really felt like she was sharing *life* with me.

A dear friend of mine sent me a treasure trove of postcards before cancer ended her life too soon. Between bouts of chemotherapy, Janne traveled to Europe and China on vacations and sent postcards to me in prison at every stop along the way. When each trip was over, I filled a manila envelope with her sequentially numbered the postcards and offered to share the postcard vacations with my prison sisters. At one point, the waiting list to read the postcards was thirty persons long! Sharing vicarious experiences gives hopes, inspires dreams, and provides mental escape from the horrors and pain of incarceration.

One more thing, by sharing these details, you are actually helping prisoners prepare for an eventual return to society. The world changes, sometimes very rapidly. The more prisoners know about those changes the better able they are to adapt, with less stress, when they leave prison. This holds true even when ministering to those who have been sentenced to "life without possibility of parole" (LWOP). A prison sister of mine, who served thirty-seven years on such a sentence, was recently granted clemency by the governor and released by the parole board. This very morning, she will be leaving CIW behind and starting a new life.

A final reason that it is important to share experiences is that you are helping prisoners to form realistic expectations. I already brought up this topic in the previous chapter as a communication gap, but it bears repeating. Church members know that life rarely runs smoothly, that individual churches may have deep divisions and issues, that sometimes God does not seem at all near when we need him the most. But when volunteers present only a positive picture of church and of life in Christ, prisoners can form the wrong expectations. And when their expectations are not met in the free world, it can lead to grave disappointment and discouragement. It can even contribute to recidivism.

I briefly mentioned the concept from Paul that we are to be "ambassadors for Christ" (2 Cor 5:20), but I want to build on that here. Merriam Webster defines ambassador as "an authorized representative or messenger" or "an unofficial representative." As prison ministry volunteers, especially those who physically enter institutions, you are both an official ambassador for Christ and an unofficial ambassador of the free world. Prisoners are looking to you to provide a link to the world outside. We are afraid that the world is changing and that we won't recognize it when we return, a fear that is often well founded. We are looking to you to provide us a realistic picture of the world beyond the institutional walls.

Care for our Families

One of the most frustrating aspects of incarceration is the powerlessness in terms of our being able to care for our loved ones. How do I describe my own anguish at not being able to care for my mother as she fought her way through radiation and chemotherapy? I already touched on the difficulties that incarceration places on parent-child relationships. Angel Tree, Get on the Bus, and similar ministries do inestimable good by helping to transcend this gap and are highly valued by incarcerated parents. Angel Tree supplies Christmas gifts to the children of incarcerated persons in the parent's name. Get on the Bus is a California ministry that transports children and a guardian to distant prisons to visit parents.

You may have a very difficult time understanding just how powerless incarcerated people are within their familial relationships. One mother I talked with expressed pain and frustration over the responses she received when she went to ministry volunteers requesting prayer for a teenage daughter who was pregnant. In addition to prayer, this heartbroken mother received unasked for advice about what she should do, including being told to show "tough love." The problem was that this prisoner was powerless to do *anything* except pray! So instead of providing comfort and strength through prayer, what the ministry volunteer did was shape prayer to emphasize the mother's helplessness, powerlessness, and failure as a parent.

A Chance to Give Back

Those who have been incarcerated need an opportunity to give back. Restorative justice is not just about trying to find a way to not be imprisoned. The perpetrator needs the opportunity to offer apology, experience and provide healing, and work towards restoration of relationship. Crimes cannot be undone, but repentant perpetrators need to be allowed to make meaning of their lives by contributing.

Within institutions, this can be accomplished by finding a need that is within the prisoners' ability to meet. At CIW, women who work in the prison sewing factory by day, meet one evening a week in that same factory to donate their efforts to Happy Hats, a program that fabricates fun, colorful hats for children hospitalized with cancer. Groups raising and training dogs to provide mobility and other support for disabled persons realized that prisoners were willing and able to do this. One church donated yarn to a prison that resulted in prisoners crocheting blankets for orphanages and disabled veterans.

Contrast the above with the experience of my friend who tried to volunteer at a church after she left prison. The church told her that they already had enough volunteers and did not need her. She was devastated. This is not how a church makes returning prisoners feel welcomed, accepted, and appreciated for their gifts.

Mentors and Friends

Prisoners and former prisoners need mentors and friends. Research has shown that ex-prisoners who had contact with mentors from voluntary agencies do significantly better than those who do not (Brown and Ross 2010). A mentoring relationship helps to create and restore the social fabric while providing needed social capital to facilitate prisoners transition to freedom (Koschmann & Peterson 2013).

One of the examples of a successful mentoring program, M2 (Match Two) Prison Ministry matches a community volunteer with a man or woman incarcerated in a prison (M2W2 2019). The purpose is one-on-one Christian mentoring through monthly visits. Volunteers meet with their assigned match as part of a group. During the group time, volunteers and inmates visit as they might over a cup of coffee. Men meet with men in men's prisons. Women meet with women in women's prisons.

The relationships developed in this context are very different than what usually develops during church services. First of all, prisoner and volunteer spend considerable time together, at least once a month and often several hours at a time in one-on-one interpersonal communication, building relationship. In this context, and unlike interactions with other prison ministry volunteers, it was expected that both prisoner and volunteer/mentor would share some personal information. Finally, it was intended that these relationships continue after the release of the prisoner. None of these factors are usually present in other prison ministry volunteer/prisoner interactions.

I personally know the value of having a Mentor. My Mentor visited me in prison for several hours at least once a month for a decade, and established a relationship with me while I was in prison. It was my Mentor who heard my heart's desire to attend graduate school someday, found the Fuller Theological Seminary Certificate of Christian Study program, and helped me enroll as a distance-learning student. My Mentor waited at the prison gate with a long-stemmed rose to welcome me to the free world upon my release, and she has actively mentored me ever since. My current work would not be possible without all the ways that my Mentor heard me and supported me for the last twenty years. Heartbreakingly, the mentoring programs at the California Institution for Women have expired due to lack of support and funding.

Discussion Questions

1. What did you find most surprising about what prisoners need and ask for? Why was this surprising?

2. What do you believe that the Church has to offer prisoners that other social service resources cannot offer?

3. How is God calling you to use your power as an advocate for prisoners?

4. How might more mentoring programs be instituted for currently and formerly incarcerated persons? How could your church contribute to this effort?

Chapter 7

Theories of Prison Ministry: An Historical Perspective

Why do we approach prison ministry the way we do in the U.S.? Is prison ministry only about reforming prisoners, or might reforming the prison system also be part of prison ministry? How and why did the U.S. end up with the kind of prison and jail structures that we currently see in place? These are some of the questions we will be addressing in this chapter. There is almost universal agreement that our system does not work; it neither protects society nor provides racial equity. But until we understand how we got where we are, it is going to be prohibitively difficult to move forward.

European presence in Colonial America was initially a direct extension of European culture, and English power structures. It is important to remember that European settlers were forcibly imposing this culture on pre-existing peoples with vastly different cultural values, especially in terms of "crime." Prisons and jails did not exist in what is now the U.S. prior to the introduction of European culture. Traditional indigenous methods of conflict resolution (which included traditional dispute resolution, peacemaking, talking circles, family or community gatherings, and traditional mediation) were consistent with methods of restorative and reparative justice (Melton 2005). These Native American systems were generally based on restoring harmony and peace to the victim and community, while still including elements of accountability (Jweied 2014). However, European culture quickly became the dominant structure, and subdominant indigenous methods were perceived as irrelevant. Thus, in Colonial America prior to the late 1600s, prisons and jails were based, not surprisingly, on contemporary English practices. Therefore, in order to provide a backdrop for this chapter, I will begin with a brief overview of English prisons of that time period.

English Models

Originally, English prisons, like most prisons from biblical times onward, were not intended for punishment, penitence, or rehabilitation. Rather, prisons were places to hold those persons who were either awaiting trial, were political prisoners, or were unable to repay their debts. The actual punishment for crimes consisted mainly of corporal punishment such as flogging, dismemberment, or death (Graber 2008, 19).

One of the most notorious of England's prisons, Newgate Prison, was built as a result of Henry II's instigation of legal reforms giving the Crown more authority in administering justice (Halliday 2007). Here, sheriffs and jailers made their living from fees collected from prisoners for supplying such services as applying and removing shackles, and from supplying such goods as food and beds. Well before the British colonization of Australia with convicts, England was engaged in the practice of using prisoners to colonize America. In the early 1600s, vagrancy was criminalized in England for the specific intention of increasing the number of prisoners who were then shipped off to help populate the new world with cheap labor (Christianson 1998). However, the American Revolution ended convict transports from England to the U.S., which then (over) filled English jails with vagrants, debtors, and those awaiting trial.

This was the situation when, in the eighteenth century, the Calvinist John Howard began to institute prison reforms in England. As High Sheriff, Howard was appalled to find out that many prisoners remained locked up after they were acquitted of crimes because they could not afford to pay the jailer's fees (Chapman 2013). Howard advocated such reforms as the abolition of jailer fees, providing decent food and clothing to prisoners, and separating women prisoners from male prisoners. Unfortunately, Howard was more successful at describing the need for reform than at actually implementing it. (Chapman 2013, 548-9).

Early North American Prison Models

The process by which colonial America gradually asserted its independence from England and English culture resulted in a divergence from English common law (Acevedo 2012).

In Colonial America, the methods employed for the punishment for crimes had a two-fold purpose. First, the criminal was discouraged from committing more crimes by punishments that usually involved shaming. Second, the criminal was restored to community, often after a public confession and apology for offenses committed. This was possible in a radically smaller world, where criminals were generally known by the entire community and not readily able to move to any community where they would not be known. A sentence to labor for the benefit of the community was easily enforced and neither confinement or policing was necessary (Adamski 2012, 2032). Ultimately, a dichotomy emerged with the growth of slavery in the South and with industrialization in the North.

The North: The growth of northern cities meant that small community shaming and restoration techniques were no longer effective in dealing with crimes. Instead, workhouses were instituted where criminals sentenced to labor were incarcerated, both to protect the community and to remove them from the community.

William Penn was the first great American Quaker prison reformer. In his "Great Experiment" in Pennsylvania in the 1680s he abolished capital punishment for all crimes except murder. He also believed that prisons should be workhouses, that bail should be allowed for minor offences, and that prisoners should not have to pay food, lodging or other fees (Quakers 2020). He had a view towards rehabilitation, believing that prisoners should be helped to learn a trade to increase their ability to make an honest living upon release. These were radical reforms for the time, putting into practice Penn's Quaker faith in equality and the possibility of nurturing 'that of God' in everyone. In this Pennsylvania model, the Quakers believed, the reformation of criminals would best be accomplished through solitary confinement, which would provide time and opportunity for self-reflection and contrition (Schmid 2003).

For decades, two systems were held in opposition in the United States, the Pennsylvania system and the Auburn system. The Pennsylvania model was based on the belief that criminals could best be reformed through solitary confinement, which was intended to provide time and opportunity for self-reflection and contrition. The choices that Pennsylvania Quakers made in the building of their ideal prison, the Eastern State Penitentiary which opened in 1829, from its architecture to its operating principle of "reformation through solitary confinement," were informed by their theological beliefs in the presence of God in every person and their understandings of human nature. The alternate model was developed in New York, referred to as the corporate system or Auburn system. The Auburn prison opened in 1817, with prisoners sleeping in tiny cells at night but working together during the day while under a strictly enforced rule of silence.

These original prison reforms of the early 1800s in America were, in themselves, models of prison ministry. These reforms answered the question "How should the church minister the gospel message to those who commit crimes?" But by the end of the century, the thinking behind these reforms was falling out of favor. Not only was modernist thought looking at human nature in more scientific terms while religious perspectives were deemed superstitious, but both the Pennsylvania and Auburn systems were getting out of hand. By 1897 Eastern State Penitentiary housed 1200 prisoners in just 765 cells, although solitary confinement was not officially abandoned until 1913 (Schmid 2003).

The South: While I refer to the actual prison reforms in the northeastern U.S. as prison ministry, the same cannot be said about confinement of prisoners in the southern states. Slavery as an institution had provided slave owners with the power to punish behaviors perceived to be against the interests of the non-slave community. In 1669 Virginia wrote a statute that exempted slave owners from prosecution "should they 'chance' to kill a slave during the 'extremity' of 'correction'"(Waldrep2011). In fact. the first *uniformed* police force in the U.S. was formed in Charleston, NC in the 1780s as a response to complaints about slaves congregating in towns (Waldrep2011).

Here the "workhouse" aspect of prison was emphasized to the extreme. Prisons were intentionally heavily populated by detaining African Americans for the sole purpose supplying free labor to replace that lost by the formal abolishment of slavery. The practice of "convict leasing" was implemented, whereby sheriffs made profit by leasing the labor of black men to companies who had little investment in the laborers (Blackmon 2008). While slave owners had an economic investment in slaves, those who leased convict labor had no economic motivation to feed or maintain the lives of these prisoners. There was no care of bodies or souls in this system. Prisons and jails were money making enterprises that depended on a constant influx of Black bodies.

Prison Reform vs Prison Abolition

Prison reform is a major topic in the U.S. today. Various groups have various ideas and priorities for what this means. On their website, the ALCU lists their priorities for prison reform *(https://www.aclu.org/other/aclu-policy-priorities-prison-reform)* as being:

1. Reduction in incarceration,

2. Improvements in conditions of confinement,

3. Emphasis on rehabilitation and treatment programs,

4. Halt transfers of child offenders to adult facilities,

5. Attention to concerns of female prisoners,

6. Decriminalization of mental illness, and

7. Elimination of private prisons.

All of these are goals towards making prison more humane. These are issues that need immediate addressing. However, are these reforms enough?

The biggest problem with the idea of prison reform is the underlying assumption that the current system can be fixed. Reform is one of those "re" words that implies that what already exists can be "restructured" or "remade" to be more effective. However, the argument is made by some that our current prison system is actually working incredibly efficiently at achieving the goal of maintaining social inequality. The racial underpinnings of our current system were deliberately conceived in order to exploit African Americans for labor.

"Abolition" as a topic generally refers to the freeing of slaves in the U.S. under the 13th Constitutional Amendment which states: Neither slavery nor involuntary servitude, except as a punishment for crime whereof the party shall have been duly convicted, shall exist within the United States, or any place subject to their jurisdiction. However, the documentary film *13th* argues that this amendment that purportedly ended slavery, instead created a new form of slavery through incarceration. In this way, abolition of prisons can be seen as a continuation of the struggle to end slavery in the U.S.

Angela Davis, a noted scholar, activist, writer, and Distinguished Professor Emerita of History of Consciousness and Feminist Studies at UC Santa Cruz, was incarcerated for a year before being acquitted of all charges and a leading proponent of prison abolition. Davis says of prison abolition that, "Abolitionist approaches ask us to enlarge our field of vision so that rather than focusing myopically on the problematic institution and asking what needs to be changed about that institution, we raise radical questions about the organization of the larger society"(2003). She further explains that "For centuries, people have been unwilling to grasp the concept that only by undoing the foundation can we build a new future"(Davis 2020).

Appallingly little has changed in the last two hundred years. Prison factories still make profits by working prisoners at far below minimum wage. At CIW where I was incarcerated, prisoners could earn up to $1 per hour working in the sewing factory. A 2020 article, tellingly titled "California Is Blaming Prison Reform for Incarcerated Fire Fighting Labor Shortage," estimates that the state saves $100 million a year by relying on prison labor, paying incarcerated firefighters up to $5.12 per day with an additional $1 per hour when actively fighting a fire (Funes 2019).

We continue to secure individuals in locked facilities, removed from community. Overcrowding ensures that the solitude for reflection that was the Quaker reformers' intent is not achieved. But no new model has been developed. Now, prison ministry generally consists of teams or individuals from nearby churches entering the jails and prisons to bring Bible studies and services to the incarcerated.

1. What is your evaluation of the Quaker model of "Penitentiaries?" What were the positive aspects and what were the negative repercussions?

2. What do you think might be possible connections between "convict leasing" and the current trend towards privatization of prisons?

3. What prison reforms do you believe should be of highest priority? Why did you choose these?

4. How do you respond to the idea of prison abolition? How might society might respond to crime without relying so heavily on prisons?

5. In the first paragraph it stated that "until we understand how we got where we are, it is going to be prohibitively difficult to move forward." How does what you now understand about the history of prisons in the U.S. affect how you will now move forward?

Chapter 8

Prison Theology

This chapter will offer insights into prison theology in a way that will help you in the next chapter to develop your own theology of prison ministry, hopefully one that is grounded in redemption.

Yes, prisoners have their own theology! Remember, theology really means taking a deep look into who God is and how He works within a specific context. The matter of context is important because how we see God, and what we need from God, is shaped by the circumstances and culture in which we find ourselves. So just as a hungry person looks to God for bread and a thirsty person looks to God for water, a guilty person looks to God for redemption.

Difference Between Theology of Prison Ministry and Prison Theology

Before you take on the challenge of formulating your own theology of prison ministry in the next chapter, an important distinction must be made. Theology of prison ministry is **not** the same as prison theology! Because God is already in prisons, prison theologies exist: specific contextualizations of the gospel that give meaning to the pain of crime, sin, victimization, and incarceration in each jail and prison. Prison theology is about how prisoners think of their condition, community and whole life span in light of their experience of God and the gospel. Still, while prison theology and theology of prison ministry are not the same, they are inexorably linked. That is why I am devoting a full chapter to each. That is why I am devoting a full chapter to each. My hope in sharing with you my personal theology is that once you have an idea of what one prisoner's theology looks like, you will have a framework upon which to build your own theology of prison ministry.

My experience has been that prison theology originates within prison and prisoners. This means that prison theology is not something that can be imposed or formulated by outsiders such as chaplains, volunteers, or any other well-meaning person who has never been incarcerated. Further, it is very seldom that prisoners are asked or allowed to share their theological standpoint. And often, when prisoners do try to share, they are either dismissed or "corrected" and told their theologies are wrong. So here, as someone who for 30 years lived, studied, and ministered as a prisoner, I will share my theological insights and positions, which I admittedly do with a gendered perspective. I do not presume to speak for all prisoners, not even all women prisoners, in discussing prison theology. Instead, I intend to provide a basic survey of topics and issues that have been important to me and hope that this will be helpful to you as you grapple with your own theology of prison ministry.

Gender

Not all prisoners at CIW, have always identified themselves or been identified by others as women. For instance, transgender persons in various stages of gender change are incarcerated, and the guidelines for who is sent where in a binary prison system can be very arbitrary. I have witnessed volunteers who were shocked and did not know how to react to transgender prisoners, whispering afterwards amongst themselves of the "He/She" who attended service. If I heard the whispers, undoubtably others did too. And I am certain that the subject of the whispers knew, at the very least, of the lack of acceptance and grace that was being offered them. I have also known a transgender sister who became fully respected as an elder and a worship leader within the CIW Christian community. These experiences have caused me to examine, and periodically re-examine, my biases and prejudices regarding gay, transgender, and non-binary gendered persons. As a result, my abiding conviction is that "What God has made clean, you must not call profane" (Acts 10:15), and that these persons are my fully redeemable and beloved sisters and brothers in Christ.

Contextual Diversity in Prison Theology

There is no one single prison theology since each prison is unique. At the California Institution for Women (CIW) alone, congregations from various parts of the prison differed radically in contexts, needs, and theologies. The Reception Center houses only new or returning prisoners who are dealing with identity issues and traumas associated with crisis. The Support Care Unit houses diagnosed psychiatric patients, a context in which demons and spiritual warfare are of immanent concern. In the 1980s, when the diagnosis of AIDS was a two-year death sentence, the closed HIV+ Unit prisoners were focused more on eschatology, on end times, and what life after death looks like. Spanish speaking Latina services contextualize for both prison and Hispanic culture. Finally, and of vital importance, is contextualization for gender. Prison is not gender neutral, prison theology is not gender neutral, and prison ministry is certainly not gender neutral.

The "W" in CIW stands for women, and the majority of these women are mothers. I have witnessed, and experienced, the pain that well-intentioned but ill prepared prison ministry volunteers can cause by repeating the same Mother's Day sermon that had been so well received in their home church.

Churches will be better able to understand their relationship to prisoners if they understand prisoners' relationship to God, to Jesus, and to the Holy Spirit as well as to the Church. Prison taught me that:

- I need an all-powerful God who is bigger than my circumstances,
- I need Jesus to be fully human and fully God so he understands my circumstances and still has the authority to forgive me,
- I need the abiding presence of the Holy Spirit and the Spirit's wisdom to help me through each day's struggles, and
- I need to be in healthy relationships with fellow believers in the church.

I will be talking about my prison theology by using five of the 12 academic categories of traditional systematic theology: theological anthropology, Christology, ecclesiology, pneumatology, and eschatology. These systematic theology categories simply give me a framework upon which to hang my thoughts, and purists will note that I have taken liberties and lumped categories together where it suits my purpose. That purpose is to give you points of reference, to provide you with some vicarious experiences, that sum up my thirty years of living in prison as a Christian. Most people to whom you minister will be neither so systematic in their understandings, nor so worried about theology.

Theological Anthropology

I will begin with theological anthropology, the study of the relationship between God and humans, or "Who does God say we are?" The short answer lies in the imago dei, in the idea that humans were created in the image of God (Gen. 1:26-27). Strangely enough, this concept is easier for me to apply to others than it is to apply to myself. While the Bible tells me beyond dispute that humans were created in God's image, I have two issues in applying this to myself. Firstly, I have been convicted of an inhuman crime. Secondly, I endured thirty years of dehumanizing incarceration. It is only by hanging on desperately to the biblical truth that God has provided for my redemption that I can hope to see in myself any reflection of God's image.

However, I am absolutely convinced that the image of God is fully evident in all people, without regard to ethnicity, race, skin color, gender, or any other artificial boundary applied to exclude others. While my experience in a women's prison may not reflect the experiences of those in men's prisons, prison has had me live in close quarters (or even the same cell) as Black, White, Native American, Hispanic, and Asian sisters, as well as the severely mentally ill, and, without exception, I have seen the love-light of Jesus' face in all of them.

God and retribution and punishment: The concept of retribution is certainly biblical. The Old Testament formulates it as the principle of an eye-for-an-eye and a tooth-for-a-tooth (Ex. 21:24). However, we too often forget that in the New Testament Jesus specifically addresses and negates this principle (Matt. 5:38-41). There is never an excuse for retributive justice in Christianity when the entire New Testament is taken as a whole; Jesus never gives place or acceptance to the violence of punishment.

We also overlook that God says, "Vengeance is mine, I will repay" (Deut. 32:35, Rom. 12:19, Heb. 10:30). Likewise, only once in New Testament scripture is punishment administered by someone other than God (2 Cor. 2:6-11). Even here, Paul admonishes the church at Corinth to forgive and console the offender. The radical and subversive love of Christ, even for prisoners, stands in stark contrast to the current incarcerative practices of our government. I do want to make clear that I understand that some persons are simply too dangerous to allow them access to the public. I have met fellow prisoners whose potential release frightened me; I did not want these persons living in proximity to my family! However, I still saw Jesus' face in them, could see glimmers of the person God created each of them to be, and could find love for them. In Chapter 10, we will look at how there might be different options than prison. There needs to be accountability for our actions, but accountability does not have to mean simply punishment and retribution. Rev. Dr. Robert Bertram, in a Vietnam War era article titled "On the Care and Feeding of Enemies (Rom 12:16b-21), wryly points out that, if in spite of God's "monopoly on retribution you still insist on competing with Him, then your chances of winning in that sort of competition are frankly not encouraging" (1971, 319).

Christology

Christology is how we each answer Jesus' question "Who do you say I am?" Christology is our understanding of who Christ is and what he does. When prisoners answer this question there is no artificial boundary between ontology, who Christ Jesus is, and praxis, what His incarnation, death, and resurrection accomplish, past, present, and future, in creation and in the lives of believers. This holistic approach to Christology deeply informs my theology.

Christ is Son of God and Christ is Son of Man: Decades as a prison/lay minister have shown me that I am not the only prisoner who has been comforted by the injunction to "lean not on your own understanding" (Prov. 3:5b) and who therefore, without any doubt as to its validity, attributes the dual, fully God/fully human, nature of Jesus to mystery. Very few prisoners are acquainted with the classic theological arguments of Athanasius and Arius in the third century regarding the humanity and divinity of Christ (fodder for most seminary students). However, to many who are incarcerated it is still obvious that if Jesus is not fully God, he does not have the power to save us, and that if Jesus is not fully human, he cannot understand our sinful condition (Karkkainen 2003, 70). Therefore, while the ancient metaphysical arguments may not be immediately relevant to prisoners, the resultant understanding of Jesus' dual human/divine nature is vitally so.

Christ is our Redeemer: (Heb. 9:12-15, Rom. 3:24, I Cor. 1:30, Eph. 1:7, Col. 1:14) The historic sense of redemption involved securing someone's release through payment, for example, prisoners of war or those who sold themselves into slavery to pay off a debt (Is. 35:10) so that the death of Christ allows believers to be free from slavery to the law or to death, in order that they might become servants of God instead.

Redemption from the Pawnbroker

I found an understanding of redemption that was easy to explain and relevant to the congregations in prison; I expanded upon the pawnbroker metaphor.

He it is who gave himself for us that he might redeem us from all iniquity and purify for himself a people of his own who are zealous for good deeds. (Titus 2:14)

Many of us in prison know what it is to hock something to a pawnbroker. We have had something of value, and we really needed money, maybe for drugs, maybe just to feed our children. So, we gave the pawnbroker the ring or guitar, while we received less cash than it was really worth along with a pawn ticket. But somehow, we never had enough money to redeem the ticket, to buy back the ring or guitar, before the time limit expired. We cannot come up with the currency to buy them back; no matter how hard we try, we just end up further in debt. Someone else, who had the cash ended up owning what was ours, and we could never get it back.

This is not unlike what happens to our souls through sin. We know that we have all sinned (Rom. 3:23) and the wages of sin is death (Rom. 6:23). So, think of the devil as a pawnbroker, who can "destroy both soul and body in hell" (Matt. 10:28). When we sin it is like we turn over our soul to him for whatever it was our flesh needed. But now we do not have, nothing we have is valuable enough, to buy back our soul. Time is running out on our tickets, and if they are not redeemed, we will permanently forfeit our souls.

But if we come to Jesus, who has obtained through his death on the cross and resurrection the currency needed, he redeems our souls. Jesus pays the pawnbroker, and frees us from our sins by his blood (Rev. 17:6). He restores our souls (Ps. 23:3).

This is my prison theology which, as already stated, is not the same as a theology of prison ministry. But you need to be exposed to this understanding of what redemption means because prisoners know that they are sinners. While many lifetime congregation members sometimes need to be reminded that they are sinners, the challenge in ministering to those who have been convicted of crimes is quite the opposite. Prisoners need to be convinced that we are salvageable, redeemable.

Unfortunately, my experiences tell me that not all prison ministry team members are convinced that redemption extends to all prisoners. How can the church be effective in ministering redemption to prisoners if prison ministry is not thoroughly grounded on the key biblical belief that redemption extends even to the guiltiest criminal? Redemption all boils down to this: Do we really believe that every person is redeemable?

Christ is the Redeemer of All Creation: You might be wondering why I make this a separate topic when we have just discussed Christ as our Redeemer. I do so because this understanding is of inestimable value in ministering to those who are unsure of their humanity. According to Romans 8:19-23, Christ Jesus redeems more than just humans; he is the redeemer of all creation. Many prisoners know that we have acted inhumanely and believe we have forfeited our humanity, a view that is often reinforced by the correctional system. For example, while preparing a report about me for an impending parole board hearing, a Correctional Counselor once said to me, "Even a dog knows how to protect its young. How do you explain that you allowed your daughter to be killed?" At this point, what does redemption in Christ have to do with me if redemption only applies to humans? The healing process that culminates in a prisoner believing in her/his own humanity may be lengthy and difficult. It may, in some cases, be entirely impossible without the kind of intervention by God that can only be called a miracle.

Christ is our Atonement (Rom. 3:25, Heb. 2:17): What "atonement" actually means is a topic that theologians have endlessly debated. Various models have gained and lost popularity through the centuries (such as ransom theory, satisfaction theory, penal substitution, Christus Victor, Moral influence theory, and Girard's scapegoat theory) and each has something of value to offer us in the development of a theology of prison ministry. I am not going to discuss any of those here, but rather to acknowledge that each is an attempt to explain the absolute truth that the Bible overflows with metaphors and images of the atoning work of Jesus Christ. I want to present here that, while it is not all that popular in mainline churches, my experience is that penal substitution is a metaphor of atonement that is particularly relevant and helpful within the context of prison ministry. In penal substitution, sin is equated with crime, and in Jesus' work on the cross he substituted himself and paid the penalty for our crime. Ultimately, the atoning work of Jesus results in the redemption of sinners, and extends, most meaningfully, even to prisoners.

Christ is our Freedom (John 8:36, 2 Cor. 3:17): The connection between freedom in Christ and prison ministry seems rather obvious. But if this aspect of Christology is not adequately developed, it can be terribly counterproductive. It is a 'no-brainer' that most prisoners desire freedom. However, I have seen too many prisoners turn away from the Church due to misunderstanding what freedom in Christ means, believing that freedom means a change in physical circumstances. While it is true that sometimes God performs a miracle that results in an early release from prison or jail for a prisoner, as a rule, this is not how things work out.

Early release was certainly not the case in my own experience. As I have mentioned previously, the first ten times that the parole board found me suitable for parole, the various California governors used their veto power to reverse parole, even though the prison church, the ministry volunteers, and I were all praying for my physical freedom. I came to see that Jesus was instead granting me the freedom to serve him within my experiences in prison. However, I have seen more than one prison ministry volunteer face a severe crisis of faith when God did not grant their prayers for *my* release in the timeframe that they were expecting.

This leads us to the two important questions must be asked about what it means that Christ is our freedom: freedom from what, and freedom to do what? For the first, prisoners no longer need to be slaves to sin, slaves to whatever masters us (Acts 13:39, Rom. 6:18-23, 2Pet. 2:19). This may mean addictions, relationships, or old thought and behavior patterns. Prisoners are also free from the fear of death (Heb. 2:15). As for what prisoners are free to do, we are free in Christ to love and serve one another (Gal. 5:13). Shockingly for many prisoners, this means free to love those who have harmed us, to love those who hold us prisoner, and to love even ourselves.

Christ is our Restorer: Restoration is a topic far more significant to those who know how much they have lost than to those who have never really experienced loss. The loss of relationships, health, and positive self-image often results in the loss of hope.

Christ restores relationships. Too often in individualistic Western Christianity, the restoration of relationship with God is understood to be primarily a personal event, something occurring between the believer who is saved and restored, and God the Father. While not untrue, this narrow view omits that our triune God, whose very nature is community, restores believers to his Body, which is also community by its very nature. Restoration of prisoners to relationship within the prison church is only a first step. We must think beyond the restoration of the new believer's relationship with God, including restoring their relationships with family, with society in general through release, and even inclusion in the churches in the community.

Christ restores mental and physical health. Sin and crime can be as devastating to prisoners' physical and emotional health as it is to their spiritual health. Thus, another important aspect of Christology for prisoners involves when mentally ill prisoners come to understand that Jesus restored the Gerasene demoniac, (Mark 5:1-20), Mary Magdalene (Luke 8:20, 7:21), and others to their right minds. Christ gives hope to all who struggle with both emotional and physical distress. Prison is not a healthy environment at best, and prison medical care is notoriously bad (Talvi, Silja J. A. 2007, 89-90). In addition to this, many prisoners had lifestyles prior to their incarceration that harmed their health. Whether the issue is HIV and hepatitis from needle sharing and other risky behaviors, the poor nutrition that may be associated with poverty and/or lifestyle choices, or the abuses upon bodies that are the result of violence, prisoners rely on the possibility of healing and the restoration of health in Christ Jesus.

Christ is our restorer of purity. That this aspect of Christ's person and work is under-represented to prisoners, specifically women prisoners, was made astonishingly real to me while I was still in prison. As part of an assignment for a Fuller Seminary distance learning class, I interviewed the women of CIW's Muslim community. All but one of these women had converted to Islam (from nominal Christianity) while in prison, and over half of them volunteered that a major contributing reason was that Islam, through practices of prayer, fasting, and modesty, provided an avenue for restoring their purity that they had not found within

Christianity. I, like these other women, had never heard a sermon that satisfactorily dealt with the issue of purity.

Although Jesus is not specifically addressed as the restorer of purity, Scripture supports this understanding. When the woman with the issue of blood touched Jesus, she had been ritually impure for 12 years (Luke 8:43-48). By making her healing public, Jesus restored her purity in the sight of her community. Peter was told by God not to call unclean what God himself had made clean (Acts 10:15). Jesus washed the disciples' feet and called them clean (John 13:3-10). Further, Scripture says that former sinners have been washed and sanctified (1Cor. 6:11). Therefore, Christ as the restorer of purity is an important aspect of a theology of prison ministry.

Christ is our restorer of hope. Hope can be a very hard sell to prisoners. Simultaneously, hope may be all that a prisoner has. Still, 1 Corinthians 15:19-20 says Christ is our hope not only for this life, but also for the one to come. It is only when hope is understood as a subject, not an object, that hope becomes a vital force. Ray Anderson recognized this when, in his last book *The Seasons of Hope,* he cited a letter I had written to him from prison in which I explained, "I will not always get what I hope for, but I will never be disappointed by hoping in Christ" (Anderson 2008, 80-1).

Ecclesiology

Prison theology has its own understanding of ecclesiology, the relationship of prisoners to Church and churches. I have had to learn the difference; to distinguish between the *Church* (singular), the entire body of Christ and consisting of all believers across space and time, and *churches* (plural), the contextual expressions of the local congregations of believers. As I have said before, in prison we just call it all Church!

The Church is the Body of Christ (Rom. 12:5, 1 Cor. 12:12-27, Eph. 4:11-13): It is important to remember that the churches in the community and the churches in prisons are equally constituent of the Church as the Body of Christ. As mentioned earlier, it is a mistake to believe that the church in the community is bringing God to a godless place; God is already in his church within prison.

I will share here a concept that my friend Dr. Jason Sexton introduced, coining the term *ecclesia incarcerate* to refer to the church within prison (2015, 83). Having had some interactions with the judicial system as a youth, he recognizes that: within the space established by one of California's most problematic institutions is an underestimated, underrepresented and underutilized actor: the church. It exists in this unique and fixed context in which volunteers (who often do not know this context experientially) and chaplains (employees of the State) either err to impose alternate structures or else simply lack the ability to contextualize due to other real constraints. Christian theology, however, doesn't share these same impediments, since Jesus has already designated his location – the location of his body – as incarcerate (Sexton 2015, 88).

In many ways, the church in prison is closer to the church I read about in Acts 2 at the Pentecost than many churches I have experienced outside prison. In prison church there is a greater reliance upon and interdependence between members who are learning Christian beliefs (orthodoxy) and practices (orthopraxis), especially because the believers there are living under oppressive and difficult circumstances.

There is an interrelatedness between justice and mercy beyond polarity; mercy is a constituent aspect of justice. As noted earlier, this interplay is a biblical theme repeated in stories of Jesus.

Pneumatology

Pneumatology is the study of the Holy Spirit, the *pneuma* (the very breath of God). Who is the Holy Spirit to me? My understanding leans more towards the charismatic than many mainline churches are comfortable with. This is probably because I have personally experienced so much pure evil that I cannot deny the reality of dark spiritual forces.

Spirit of Christ within us (Rom. 8:9-11, 2Cor. 13:13, Phil. 1:19): The Holy Spirit is the very Spirit of Christ, of whom Jesus spoke saying it was better for his disciples that he left in order for the Spirit to come. I need only look at Peter before and after Pentecost to understand the difference that the indwelling of the Holy Spirit can make in a life.

Spirit of Truth (John 14:17, 16:3): As a general rule, prisoners are particularly well acquainted with lies, with liars, with broken promises, and other distortions of truth. It is sometimes the case that lies are so deeply embedded that a prisoner no longer has the ability to discern between lies and truth, even in his or her own thoughts. This may be due to dysfunctional family of origin, mental health issues, self-preservation on the streets, the vagaries of the social justice system, or all the above.

Spirit of Power (Eph. 3:16): Jesus promises that the Holy Spirit will bring power to believers (Acts 1:8). The first fulfillment of this promise is experienced on the day of Pentecost (Acts 2:2-4). The idea that the Spirit of power actually resides within a prisoner can have far reaching ramifications. This is because prisoners, by definition again, are those from whom power is generally withheld. Many of these same prisoners have always, in their experience, been those who are relatively powerless within the structures of American society due to ethnicity, socio-economic level, and/or gender. Therefore, power differentials influence almost every aspect of prisoner interface with others, including other prisoners (Hofstede 2009, 24).

Power is also associated with dignity; those with the former are usually afforded the latter. Thus, the indwelling presence of the Spirit of power can be an internalized source of human dignity, the sort that counters the dehumanizing effects of prison.

Spirit of Wisdom (Isa 11:2, Acts 6:3, Eph. 1:17): Many prisoners are painfully aware that they have made "stupid" mistakes and choices. And in an environment where it is difficult to think that anyone has your best interests at heart, to whom does one turn for advice? This is one more value to prisoners of the indwelling Spirit of wisdom and understanding.

Spirit of Redemption (Eph. 4:31, Rom. 8:23): It is widely accepted that redemption is one of those aspects of the Kingdom of God that is both accomplished in the incarnation, death, and resurrection of Christ and yet also an event to come on the Day of the Lord (Ladd 1993, 56). The Spirit's part in redemption is to be the seal that marks us for this redemption. Prisoners understand what it means to have an official governmental stamp that seals their fate, such as the judge's or governor's stamp on paperwork that incarcerates or frees. But in the U.S., the appeal process often results in the overturning of a judicial decision. This is as likely to affect the prosecution side as the petitioners' side. Prisoners, therefore, do not easily trust the permanence of a decision. I remind you that, of the eleven times that the parole board told me to prepare to go home, the governor reversed that decision the first ten times. I still regularly have dreams in which I'm being told that my freedom was a mistake and I am being ordered back to prison. When I wake from such a dream, it is difficult to orient myself as to whether prison or freedom is my current reality.

In this context, the value of God's seal in the form of the Holy Spirit as assurance of future redemption cannot be overstated. This is one benefit to prisoners of Pentecostal/charismatic signs, such as speaking in tongues, of the indwelling presence of the Holy Spirit in the believer, that there is a tangible confirmation that redemption is indeed intended for the outsider, in this case the guilty prisoner (Acts 8:14-17). Unfortunately, the opposite is also true; many believers suffer greatly when they do **not** see the traditional Pentecostal signs of the Holy Spirit and therefore doubt whether the Spirit is indwelling.

Spirit as Advocate (John 14:16, 26, 15:26, 16:7, I John 2:1): The concept of the Holy Spirit as advocate is another metaphor that deeply resonates with most prisoners and ex-prisoners that I know. Merriam Webster online dictionary defines advocate as "one that pleads the cause of another before a tribunal or judicial court," in other words, an attorney. By constitutional law, there is not a single prisoner who did not have access to a defense attorney prior to conviction and incarceration, so the idea of having an attorney is relevant and very personal.

There is some overlap in the above-cited scriptures as to whether our advocate is Jesus Christ or the Holy Spirit, which is the Spirit of Christ in the world sent by the Father. However, in both, the role of the Advocate is to be with us forever, to testify of Jesus, to teach, and to plead for us when we sin.

According to scripture, we have all sinned (Rom. 3:23). Further, we are informed that the crime of sin makes us deserving of the death penalty (Rom. 6:23).

Yet, how comforting is it for believers to have an Advocate, one who has never lost a case and who is closely related to the Judge? When we go before the Judge, the Advocate will make the argument that we cannot be tried for our crimes due to a double jeopardy clause. We cannot be punished twice for a crime, and someone else has already taken the blame and completed the punishment for the crime. And in closed session in the Judge's quarters, our Advocate argues that even if it means that we criminals are getting off easy, the Judge should give us mercy because we are, after all, siblings of the Advocate by a different mother.

Spirit of Adoption (Rom. 8:14-16): To stretch the former metaphor even a bit further, it doesn't matter if we have different mothers, because even prisoners are now formally adopted into the family of God, and the Holy Spirit of Truth bears witness that this is so.

Eschatology

This aspect of Christian faith looks toward the end of the present time and to the reign of Christ. Not surprisingly, prisoners are likely to have a very negative view of what their present world has to offer. Many prisoners have grown up in poverty, and been subjected to racism, violence, addiction, and myriad other painful realities. They may need more hope than that offered by simply finding in Jesus the strength to continue to endure.

Having a vision of a new world with the second coming of Christ can be of tremendous comfort to someone who is serving a life sentence or life-without possibility of parole. I personally could not have endured the pain and loss when my best friend and closest ministry partner of over 20 years died in prison from poor medical care if I did not have hope for a better world to come.

Hope for a better world to come is not enough to give us strength to meet all of life's challenges; we need hope for today. However, when hope for a change in present circumstances is exhausted, looking forward to Christ's return is of immense comfort.

1. What was the most surprising thing you learned about the prison theology presented in this chapter? Why was it surprising?

2. Which aspect of prison theology as it is presented here is most difficult for you to accept? Why?

3. What did you resonate with in this prison theology? Why?

4. How could understanding this prison theology inform your faith?

5. How do you interpret my prison theology as contextual to my prison?

Chapter 9

Forming a Contextual Theology of Prison Ministry

That last chapter was very intense, but was not intended to intimidate you. Remember, first of all, that I am one of those crazy PhD theologians. Secondly, it took three decades of reflection as a prisoner, and another decade outside prison after that, to formulate my personal prison theology. Most importantly, I could not have done so without the hundreds of volunteers who ministered to me along the way. Untrained volunteers still do (measurably) good work. However, how much better could it be if those involved in prison ministry received some basic training! For one thing, if you have not explored what you really think about Jesus, and what you see your calling(s) to be, you will be ill prepared to answer the questions you will invariably be asked by those you minister to. And I guarantee you will be asked questions!

At its most basic level, theology is simply how we think about God. Our theologies are understandings that develop as we experience God and life. We all have thoughts about who God is, what God does, and how we relate to God. However, many of us have not thought about what we think about God, especially in a systematic way. We also have to keep in mind that theology is, of necessity, contextual. What do I mean by "contextual theology?" In reality, we are all theologians, with our own personal theologies. Thus, there is a distinction between your personal theology and a theology of prison ministry. Theology of prison ministry is messy, interacting as it does with prison theology, with systematic theology themes, and with specific contexts of the individual churches as well as the particular prison facility(ies) within their context. Therefore, theologies of prison ministry are likely to be as diverse as the contexts of the individual churches in the community.

Your personal theology deals with how it is that you experience God in your life and places of need. Our life contexts affect how we think about God. Culture, socioeconomic circumstances, race, and environment are just some of the aspects that affect our life experiences and influence how we think about God. However, a theology of prison ministry looks at how you understand God's calling to the church to minister to those impacted by mass incarceration. Who are you called to minister to? Again, context is everything. There are differences between men and women, children and adults, criminals and victims, the currently incarcerated, and the formerly incarcerated. Further, theology is not static, but something continuously emerging as we grow into new experiences. For these reasons, I cannot simply provide a theology of prison ministry that fits all churches and ministry teams. A theology of prison ministry is a work that each church and each individual must do.

Thus, the task in this chapter is for you to begin thinking about two things. How will your personal understanding of Christianity and of God influence *how* you minister to those affected by mass incarceration? And how will your personal understanding of God and Christianity influence *what* you minister?

Why is a theology of prison ministry necessary?

Why is a theology of prison ministry necessary in the first place? First, and primary to the discussion, is the proposition that mass incarceration in the U.S. is a problem so immense that it affects everyone and therefore cannot be ignored. As I presented in Chapter 1, not only is the United States incarcerating more than 0.5% of our population, we incarcerate our residents at a higher rate than any other nation, and we hold 25% of the world's incarcerated people (Levad 2011). The bottom line is that, in order to be effective, the missional church must be able to read and understand its context. There is very little room for doubt that for all churches in the U.S., the context includes mass incarceration and the frequently overlooked prisoner.

Secondly, while I previously presented a biblical argument in Chapter 1 for why the Church is called to do prison ministry, each church needs its own valid biblical mandate for prison ministry to motivate the outlay of human and fiscal resources that confront mass incarceration in the U.S. demands. Churches are too often lacking in means and motivation to minister enthusiastically or effectively in prison. For example, it was explained to me that the reason one prison ministry to the California Institution for Women (CIW) had survived the cutbacks at their mega-church following the 2008 economic crash was that, because they kept such a low profile and asked for so little, the church had forgotten they exist. Their guess was that less than five percent of the congregation had any idea that the church even had a prison ministry team! Too many congregations are constrained by lack of support and resources from developing prison ministry into the powerful vehicle for healing, reconciliation, and restoration that the church could and should be contributing to society.

Thirdly, developing a robust and missional theology of prison ministry will provide direction and guidelines for the actual practice of both in-prison ministry and after-care efforts. Very few volunteers receive any formal education or training regarding the responsibilities they are entrusted with while participating in prison ministry programs. Penal institutions do not provide training or answer most ministerial types of questions.

Finally, a prison ministry theology will help churches grapple with the expanded definition of prison ministry I have argued for throughout this book. A thoughtful theological approach to prison ministry will also illuminate such topics as racial reconciliation, homelessness, immigration, and displaced persons, which have significant commonalities and overlap with prison ministry.

The following section is a series of questions intended to lead you through the process of formulating your own contextual theology of prison ministry. You will be led through the same five systematic theology topics that I addressed in Chapter 8. However, the questions are deliberately not parallel to my prison theology because I want to discourage an apples and oranges comparison between prison theology and theology of prison ministry. This is your chance to think deeply about what prison ministry really means to you.

Theological Anthropology: What does it mean to be human?

How we understand God's relationship with people is the basis of our attitudes towards, and valuing of, ourselves and others. Therefore, it is important to look at how we conceptualize the relationship between God and humans.

What does it mean that humans were created in the **imago dei**, the image of God?

____

____

____

____

How does your understanding of the **imago dei** influence how you perceive others, especially those who have been or are incarcerated?

____

____

____

____

How can you love the **imago dei**, the image of God, in another person who has committed crimes that are inhuman?

____

____

____

____

How do you reconcile both ministering to criminals and tending to the wounds of victims?

____

____

____

____

How do you define "salvation?" Is salvation a process or something that happens at a certain point in time? Why might this distinction be important in prison ministry?

____

____

____

____

Why did God create people? What does God want or require from people in general? To what is God calling you in particular?

____

____

____

____

How do you define who is or is not a believer? How does this affect your ideas about what constitutes ministry?

____

____

____

____

Christology: Who do you say that Jesus is?

In the last chapter we looked at how some prisoners understand Jesus to be at work within prisons. In particular we saw how some prisoners view Jesus Christ as: the Son of God and Son of Man, our Redeemer, the Redeemer of All Creation, our Atonement, our Freedom, and as our Restorer. Now it is your turn to think about what Christ means to you and to prison ministry.

Who do you say that Jesus is?

____

____

____

____

What does this understanding of Jesus mean to your faith? Why is this important to you?

____

____

____

____

What do you see as Jesus' role in prison ministry?

____

____

____

____

What is it that Jesus offers to believers?

____

____

____

____

What does Jesus offer to non-believers?

____

____

____

____

What does Jesus expect from you? What is your contribution to Jesus' ministry?

____

____

____

____

If you are not bringing Jesus to prison because he is already there, what is it that you are bringing?

____

____

____

____

Ecclesiology: What does "church" mean to you?

Community churches are not accidental; each church is in its specific context for the sake of fulfilling God's purpose within that geographical and cultural space. As I explained earlier, there is no community that is not in some way affected by mass incarceration. But *how* each community church is affected will be unique to that church, and therefore its responses will be unique. Whether shaped by ethnicity, culture, wealth, or geography, specific context will shape and affect the missional theology of prison ministry of each church.

What does "church" mean to you?

____

____

____

____

What is your definition of "church?"

____

____

____

____

What, if any, is the difference between "church" and "Church?" Why do you think this is so?

____

____

____

____

What activities do you see as constituting church? Why?

____

____

____

____

What people do you see as constituting church? Why?

What is the relationship between you as an individual, your church, and the church in prison or jail?

What is your view of church structure or hierarchy? Why is this important? How might this affect how you do prison ministry?

What do you understand to be the purpose of communion? Who do you believe is qualified to preside at communion? Who can partake? How do you deal with those who don't agree with you?

What should the Church's position be regarding the needs of victims of crime?

____

____

____

____

What is the Church's responsibility and position regarding the innocent prisoners? Of repentant guilty prisoners? Of unrepentant guilty prisoners?

____

____

____

____

What is the Church's responsibility regarding structural racism, especially within prisons?

____

____

____

____

What is your personal responsibility regarding racism and how does this relate to prison ministry?

____

____

____

____

Two Different Church Experiences

1. I looked online from the computer at the halfway house to which I had been paroled. I found a church that had a friendly and welcoming home page and was within two miles, what I considered walking distance. As I approached the building I saw a gentleman in the courtyard who was obviously greeting people. I walked up to him and said, "I just got out of prison two weeks ago and I am looking for a home church. It would be wrong to be less than honest to my home church, but any church that doesn't want me because I come from prison is not my home church."

He opened his arms wide, replied "Welcome home!" and gave me a big, warm hug! I did not know that Neil was the president of the congregation, or that God had recently been working on this man's heart to receive God's people joyfully. But I felt his love, his genuine joy at my being there, and this man has been a precious friend and mentor ever since. And I am still closely connected to this church.

2. Carol, a prison ministry volunteer, related a different story to me. A woman she had ministered to inside prison, Glory, was released and Carol brought her to a church service. Carol attended a mega-church where the sanctuary held almost a thousand persons. Glory was not intimidated by the crowds. In fact, she was exhilarated to be free from prison and to be worshipping with God's body outside. When the worship music got going and Glory felt the presence of God, she responded by standing and raising her hands in joyful abandon. What Carol said about this was, "This is not how we worship at my church. It was wonderful to see how into it Gloria was! Now, no one in the congregation was rude. No one told her to sit down. But everyone was looking at her strangely. I was glad to see how much Glory obviously was loving God, but she really didn't fit in. I don't think she noticed it really. She never came back to our church that I know of."

Pneumatology: What is your understanding of the person and work of the Holy Spirit?

An inadequate doctrine of the Holy Spirit can result in misunderstood or misguided Christian mission, and Protestant theology can be timid in talking about the Holy Spirit in terms of missional ministry. It is important to remember that just as Pentecostal and other charismatic movements have gained strength worldwide, this is reflected in prisons. Therefore, a strong and coherent pneumatology, one which includes discussion of spiritual gifts and manifestations, is an integral part of a theology of prison ministry.

What is your understanding of the person and work of the Holy Spirit?

____

____

____

____

What gifts of the Holy Spirit do you believe are only historical? What gifts of the Holy Spirit do you believe are evident in the present times? How do you relate to those who disagree with you about this?

____

____

____

____

Why is the Holy Spirit important to think about in terms of prison ministry?

____

____

____

____

What is your understanding of the Holy Spirit in terms of those who do not yet profess faith in Jesus?

____

____

____

____

What is the role of the Holy Spirit in salvation? In discipleship?

____

____

____

____

Eschatology: How does our future in Christ impact the present?

Sometimes the answers available in this present life are not enough. Our vision of eternity is an important resource at such a time.

What is your understanding of eternity?

____

____

____

____

Where do you find balance in living to provide God's justice and redemption in the here and now, while waiting for God's justice and redemption to come?

____

____

____

____

What is your understanding of the second coming of Christ?

____

____

____

____

What is your concept of "heaven" and of "hell"? How do these concepts affect how you live and minister?

____

____

____

____

Is it more important to you to live for the here and now, or for the world that is to come? Why? How does this relate to prison ministry?

____

____

____

____

1.   What did you find to be the most challenging aspect of formulating a theology of prison ministry? Why?

2.   How has looking at a theology of prison ministry challenged how you think about God?

3.   What do you think might have happened if Carol had stood up next to Glory during worship?

4.   Persons who have committed sex crimes are, statistically speaking, likely to re-offend. How does the church balance its position on the redeemability of all persons with its responsibility to protect its members, especially its most vulnerable members? How could it be possible to extend mission and ministry to persons who have been convicted of sexual crimes?

5.   What is your understanding of purity? Do you think purity can be restored?

Chapter 10

A New Paradigm of Prison Ministry

This chapter will explore two aspects of looking at prison ministry differently, now that you have acquired a bit more background knowledge. First, this chapter will challenge you to think about how our "criminal justice system" could be differently envisioned. Secondly, this chapter will challenge you to think differently about your personal involvement in prison ministry in terms of our expanded definition of who and what might fall under that umbrella.

A New Paradigm for Criminal Justice-- How our Criminal Justice System Could be Differently Envisioned:

Chapter 2 provided an in depth look at biblical texts, both Old Testament and New Testament, that relate to crime, criminals, and prison. In Chapter 7 we looked at the recent history of prison and prison ministry in the U.S., a reflection of current attitudes about crime, criminals, and prison. But the fact that Chapter 2 and Chapter 7 read so differently and feel so unrelated must give us pause. I argue that the reason for this discrepancy is that the church is not doing a very good job of following biblical mandates and examples relating to crime and criminals. The popular concept of prison ministry is that it consists solely of some Christian who goes to a prison or jail facility and conducts a Bible study or church service for prisoners. Additionally, many, if not most, of the people who participate in prison ministry do so without the knowledge or support of their church, in a piecemeal or "lone wolf" manner (Barkman 2020).

There is tremendous value to prison ministry as it is currently practiced; I want to make this clear! I have personally experienced the benefits. I was a new Christian with no real understanding of my faith when I began my 30-year incarceration in 1980. In the early years of my term, it was a staff chaplain who encouraged me, taught me, and pushed me to be a leader in the prison church. And the number of prison ministry volunteers who influenced and supported me during those decades is more than I can count.

However, as we noted in Chapter 1, the common definition of prison ministry has narrowed to only encompass the Bible studies and church services held within a facility of confinement. A new paradigm of prison ministry must embrace a new, expanded definition of what this entails. After all, although many who come to Christ in prison do experience the constant and abiding presence of Jesus in prison (Barkman 2020), incarcerating persons is not an effective form of evangelism and ministry.

There is an essentially universal consensus that the current prison system is broken. The differences in thought lie in how it can best be repaired or overhauled. But what the church must come to realize and accept is that this broken system is the failed experiment of the church. Prison as we know it was a reform movement instituted by the Quakers. Therefore, the church has a responsibility to propose and implement a model to replace the one that is broken. How to begin doing so is the focus of this chapter.

But actually, the issue is even deeper. If an alternative to our current criminal "justice" system could be formulated and implemented, the word prison could conceivably become outdated. That would, in turn, cause the term prison ministry to be outdated, too! Yet it is only the term, not the work that would no longer be needed. Caring for the spiritual needs of the marginalized, of those involved in criminal activity whether directly or indirectly, and for those victimized by crime would still be vital. So, for lack of a better term at present, I will still refer to that work as prison ministry even as I hope for solutions that make our current system of mass incarceration obsolete.

What could or should a new model of prison ministry look like? The inadequacies of our current system of mass incarceration is a topic coming to the forefront as our nation examines the inherent racist structure of our criminal justice system, and how prisons have become hot spots for coronavirus and other communicable infections. The privatization of prisons themselves, and of healthcare provided to prisons and jails are also matters of concern.

Firstly, I believe that the new model of prison ministry will need to embrace restorative justice practices at its core. Restorative justice, as defined by one advocate, "aims to restore the well-being of victims, offenders and communities damaged by crime, and to prevent further offending" (Liebmann 2007). This model is not a new approach, but rather a return to traditional cultural responses to crime that operate based on restoration and reparation. In most traditional systems in Africa and Asia, as well as in Celtic and Native American cultures, justice models have been "inextricably linked" to cultural and religious understandings of those affected by criminal behavior (Kenny & Leonard 2014). Thus, it is this religious component that has made restorative justice attractive to many of its proponents, such as the Mennonites and Quakers who see a practical expression of reconciliation, redemption, and forgiveness in restorative justice practices.

This holistic approach of restorative justice is already being implemented by some parts of the church, most notably by our Catholic brothers and sisters. This emerging model is consistent with Jesus' practices of healing and of restoring the sinner to community. Some advocate practicing restorative justice alone as a model, while others suggest restorative justice be integrated with rehabilitative approaches (Zernova 2007). But while restorative justice programs are being introduced into the prisons and jails, there is little evidence that the entire structure of incarceration is being addressed.

Secondly, this book was half-written before the coronavirus pandemic took over our world and thoughts. However, through this health crisis, an additional issue with the current model of incarceration has come to the forefront. Not only are prisoners at particular risk of contagion, whether of COVID-19, AIDS, tuberculosis, or norovirus,[10] but lockdowns and quarantines mirror the isolating effects of the Quaker models. This stands in total opposition to the biblical example of restoring prisoners to community.

During this coronavirus pandemic, some are advocating both early release of nonviolent criminals and non-incarceration of those charged with minor offenses. One NBC news correspondent suggests that if, due to concerns over COVID-19, the government would cease sending new admissions to jail and prisons it could be "a de facto bail and prison reform rolled together" (Bozelko 2020). Her argument is that:

> If a person who would have been sent to prison or jail during the coronavirus outbreak doesn't break the law during their dispensation, then correction has been achieved; placing them in custody later could be considered redundant. While some might object that anyone who's spared incarceration hasn't been punished, they forget that the point of punishment is changed behavior" (Bozelko 2020).

Such a paradigm, born of tumultuous times that mandate new ways of thinking, might be just what is needed in order to bring about a new model of dealing with crime. The problem is that simply sending people to jail is not mission or ministry, even if that is what the Quaker reformers were intending when they instituted our current system of incarceration.

Another object of this chapter is to help you build a paradigm of prison ministry that includes YOU! How can you do whatever (and only that which) God is calling you to do? And then, how can you do it most effectively?

Many people go into prison ministry as "Lone Wolf" volunteers. What I mean by this is that a person will feel the call of the Holy Spirit to do prison or jail ministry, and will simply jump in with both feet. Like most volunteers, the only training is that provided by the prison or jail chaplain, which mostly consists of security rules and guidelines.

---

[10] Contagions spread rapidly in prisons; the California Institution for Women where I was then imprisoned, was quarantined due to norovirus for six weeks in the spring of 2009.

Re-envisioning Prison Ministry – Where Are You Called to Get Involved?

This is a good place to revisit our expanded definition of prison ministry to discover where God's calling may be leading you and your church to participate. In Chapter 1, we looked at how prison ministry involved more types of facilities than simply prisons. We also noted that those who are currently incarcerated or recently released need ministry, and those who may have been released years ago yet are still dealing with the repercussions of incarceration. We became aware of the need to provide ministerial care for collateral sufferers from incarceration; the affected children, parents, spouses, friends, and others. And we remembered to include the too-often-overlooked victims of crime in this number. Finally, we extended the reach to include public education about mass incarceration as within the sphere of prison ministry.

Given this expanded definition of prison ministry, our next task is to look at where and how God is calling you and your church to respond. Where has God physically and spiritually situated you and your church, and why? What are the needs that God has prepared you to meet? How can you contribute to the overall wellbeing of God's body by responding to his calling?

GSLC Case Study:

One example of a church that has gone from "Lone Wolf" prison ministry to a church-wide call to prison ministry is Good Shepherd Lutheran Church (GSLC) in Claremont, California.[11] Over ten years, I watched this congregation go from a group of loving and dedicated Christians, of whom a few did independent activities associated with prison, to a congregation that has come to see their physical location near prisons and a halfway house as God's calling. In 2010, when I showed up at their door, just two weeks out of prison and having walked the two miles from the Crossroads halfway house to GSLC, I was greeted warmly. But only a few members were aware of Crossroads, and they ministered there as individuals or through community groups not associated with GSLC.

By accepting this particular parolee into their community, GSLC began a process that expanded their awareness of mass incarceration issues, exposed members to ministry opportunities, and influenced how this congregation viewed itself.

---

[11] For a more complete treatment of this case study, see my previous book, Hidden Power & False Expecations, in which I dedicate an entire chapter to this topic.

Jails: Where is your local jail? What needs related to that jail could you or ministries in your church be meeting? The possibilities include the obvious: doing personal ministry by cell visitation, providing a Bible study, or supplying the jail with Bibles and other Christian reading material. Less obvious might include meeting the needs of families impacted by a member's arrest. These needs might consist of financial support, physical support such as food and childcare, emotional support such as counseling, and finally spiritual support, finding a way to let a family know that they are precious in the sight of God.

Prisons: Are there prisons in your area? You may be surprised at the answer to this question. Communities usually do not advertise the existence of local prisons. My dear friend who lives in Chino Hills, California, often speaks of this. When a person buys a home in her modestly exclusive community, the realtor is obligated by law to mention that there is a prison nearby. There are actually three prisons within a few miles of each other: two major prisons within Chino city limits, a third one town away, and, until recently, a Youth Authority facility. However, most people who live in the area are blithely unaware of the existence of these places. Prisons, strangely enough, are nearly invisible. They are generally located on the fringes, on land that is or was considered not valuable. This contributes to the isolation of those who are confined within them. The U.S. Census counts prisoners as residing wherever their prison is located. This means that congressional districts are determined based on where prisoners are held, not on where they come from. Due to the disproportionate ratio of non-white prisoners who are thus situated in usually predominantly white areas, this results in a very real issue regarding representation. And let us not forget, prisoners are not allowed to vote.

Re-entry ministries: Whether a residential halfway house or once-a-month re-entry fair, these are places that depend on ministry volunteers to help formerly incarcerated people to adjust to life outside of prison. In Pomona, California, where I live, the local parole office holds a monthly re-entry fair that connects parolees to community resources such as mental health counseling, sober living facilities, veterans' benefits, job placement assistance, and more. Ministry also takes the form of those who offer to help "returning citizens" (I *love* this term!) get to the

Department of Motor Vehicles to get identification or drivers' licenses. Volunteers prepare and distribute bagged lunches for attendees. Halfway houses are often dependent upon donations of food, clothing, and even household appliances which help transition to independent living.

Collateral ministries: At a recent lecture series I gave on the topics in this book, some members of my church began to see the callings they were already following as related to prison ministry in ways they had not thought of recently. One woman was a newly retired principal of a continuation high school. She shared her experiences in helping students and their families cope when members of those families were incarcerated. It was an affirming eye-opener to realize that she was already doing prison ministry. Some senior members of my church identified their calling to be that of prayer warrior, holding up and supporting in prayer both the prison ministry volunteers and those they were ministering to. Another person identified her work with the local homeless community as a venue where she was in contact with many formerly incarcerated individuals. She expressed how learning about prison ministry is valuable in helping her really hear the needs of those she was already ministering to.

So how does our expanded definition of prison ministry expand opportunities for people and churches to be active in prison ministries? How can we be conduits of God's love, mercy, and justice for those impacted by our criminal justice system? Below is a non-exhaustive list of prison ministry suggestions you might consider.

1. Pen pal programs: a safe way to connect to those who are incarcerated, without having to leave your home. For the price of some stationery and a few stamps, you can be the vital human connection to both Christ's love and to the outside world.
2. Become a mentor: a more direct way to connect with someone who is or has been incarcerated, mentors walk alongside and provide spiritual, emotional, and practical support.
3. Vote: use your voting right to advocate for real justice. Remember, prisoners for the most part do not have the agency to advocate for

themselves by voting. But it we want to change our system that results in the mass incarceration of so large a portion of our population, and so disproportionately affects our non-white population, political action and voting are vital.

4. Be a prayer warrior: No special equipment or training is necessary! And you can do this from the comfort of your own bed if you so wish! But whether you are praying for specific prisoners, victims, family members, ministers or law makers, nothing is more efficacious than prayer. Invite the Holy Spirit into the individuals and situations and help the presence of God shine brighter in the dark places.

5. Find out what kinds of donations are needed for your prison ministry context.

   - Near to where I live is a used book store that either sends donated books directly to prisoners, or uses the proceeds from selling used books to pay for postage and purchase of books for prisoners throughout the U.S.

   - I am also a coordinator for a project that provides small toiletries, stationery items, and treats to every woman at CIW every Christmas. Could you contribute to, or even implement this kind of ministry at a facility near you?

   - Financial contributions are always needed. This might mean donating directly to your church's prison ministry team, or to an organization that is providing services. This could include the modestly successful businessperson who is able to channel financial success into support for prison ministry projects.

6. Recognize the previously incarcerated amongst the homeless people you minister to and talking to them about it.

7. Initiate a study group or book group that looks more deeply into justice issues.

8. Participate in groups that provide Christmas gifts to the children of incarcerated people.

9. Support a group that brings the children of incarcerated parents to visits (often for Mother's Day and Father's Day).

10. Use your voice to humanize the plight of all of those affected by our criminal justice system.

As I said, this is a non-exhaustive list. However, just as the bible tells us that there is no part of the body that is insignificant (1 Cor. 12:12-26), there is no contribution to prison ministry that is insignificant. Your contribution is valuable.

Discussion Questions

1. Who do you know who is involved in Prison Ministry? What do you now want to ask them about their experiences with Prison Ministry?

2. How can you further the understanding of Prison Ministry and its call on your church?

3. How many aspects of integrating Prison Ministry into the fabric of GSLC do you see already present at your church? Why are these significant?

Further Study Suggestions

1. Organize a group screening of the movie **13th**. I highly recommend this movie as an eyeopener to the link between our current prison system and racial inequities in U.S. culture. (There are several good study guides for the **13th** that are available on line.) How does this movie inform your understanding of prison ministry?

2. **Just Mercy** is available as both a book and a movie. Organize either a screening or a book group. Based on a true life case of the unjust conviction of a black man for murder, this account provides much fodder for thought and discussion.

Chapter 11

Complicating Issues

Yes, there are additional issues that work to complicate the whole matter of prison ministry, both the traditional inside prisons and jails form as well as our new expanded definition types of ministry.

Dealing with Institutions and Bureaucracies:

Starting with the biggest, most complicating, and most difficult of these issues, if you are doing prison ministry you will inevitably have to deal with bureaucracies. There are reasons that our dominant language includes the term "red tape" and the proverb "You can't fight city hall." Societal structures such as institutions and bureaucracies have their own self-protective ways of doing things that basically amount to having their own cultures. I am not saying that all such structures are evil. However, it is well to remember Paul's admonition, "For our struggle is not against enemies of blood and flesh, but against the rulers, against the authorities, against the cosmic powers of this present darkness, against the spiritual forces of evil in the heavenly places (Eph. 6:12).

I have people ask me all that time, when I am talking about prisons and parole, "But why do they do that? Why are the rules that way? That just doesn't make sense!" My answer is invariably, "if it makes sense, you probably aren't getting the true picture." My sisters and brothers who have experienced prison and jail usually give a knowing smile and nod. This is a truth we remind ourselves and each other about frequently. So far, I have been speaking in generalities. I am sure you would like some specific examples.

The dress codes for visiting at the California Institution for Women (CIW), where I was incarcerated for 30 years, provides a mind-bending example. At one particular time during those years (and I have to choose a particular time because the rules are always in flux), visitors were not allowed to wear T-shirts with slogans or emblems. The stated reason was because these slogans and emblems may be gang-related. Thus, my visitor told me one Fourth of July, that she had just witnessed the sergeant in charge of visiting turning away a visitor because his shirt had the American flag printed on it. Each sergeant exerts their power by deciding which rules shall be implemented and how they shall be enforced. Probably the best way to deal with this situation about visitor clothing restrictions, which is prevalent in any prison or jail, is to find out what the most conservative guidelines are, prepare one set of clothes that is most likely to always be allowable, and keep those in the trunk of your car.

These same inconsistencies are the rule outside of prison, too. For the four years that I was on parole, travel restrictions and boundaries were entirely at the discretion of my parole officer. I was assigned at least four different parole officers during that time. One said I could go anywhere within a 50-mile radius of my home. The next one said I must remain within my county even if county borders ranged from ten to 100 miles. The third said I could go anywhere within the state of California as long as I returned to my own home at night. People trying to schedule me for speaking engagements found these rules arbitrary, confusing, and inconvenient. So did I.

One more example is a Christmas project that I help coordinate where we collect and assemble items to be placed in clear gallon zip-lock bags and given to each woman incarcerated at CIW. The complication is trying to determine which items are allowable and which are considered contraband. We must get specific written permission in advance from the Warden for any exceptions to existing rules and regulations. Because we are a credible group, we are allowed to decorate the clear bags with "stickers," even though stickers are not allowed on mail entering the institution (for fear that drugs are hidden under them). We are allowed to give individually wrapped chocolate candy as long as the wrapping is not metallic.

(Metallic candy wrappers can be stuck into electrical outlets to "pop" a circuit and make a spark with which to light an illicit cigarette.) The rules go on, and those of us who were formerly incarcerated monitor what is included in the bags, not only because we know the rules, but because we simply accept them and do not push the boundaries. We know and understand that the price for pushing the nonsensical boundaries might be the loss of the program!

Dealing with Chaplains

Mostly likely, your access to those in jail or prison will be through the staff chaplains. And various reasons dealing with chaplains may prove challenging and frustrating.

Most chaplains are overworked and under-respected. Custody staff often see them as too soft on prisoners. At CIW, the full-time chaplains' main duties are:

1. Coordinating the paperwork that allows volunteer ministers to enter the institution and conduct services, studies, and events,

2. Dealing with emergencies such as death notifications to prisoners regarding their immediate family members, and

3. Screening and providing prisoner phone calls to immediate family members who are sick or dying.

4. Unfortunately, there is seldom enough time left for a chaplain to lead services, provide counseling, and provide the spiritual direction that most people presume is the job of chaplaincy.

It is important to follow the chaplains' guidelines. They have become masters of negotiating their own bureaucracy, and they know how things work. They are responsible for you and will deny you access to their institution if you cannot follow the rules. Most chaplains are very good, a few are very bad, and some are simply ineffective. But even the best will probably not have the time and resources to give you all the support you want and need, and you will need to cope with the resulting frustration. In a worst-case scenario, you will have to discern whether you can continue to minister under a particular chaplain. An example of the worst-case scenario was when the Protestant chaplain at CIW was a sexual predator. It took several years after he was repeatedly reported for inappropriate behavior before investigators discovered him in a sexually compromising situation and was terminated. In conversations after this culminating incident, several women ministry volunteers revealed that they had experienced sexual harassment and had to endure it or risk being barred from CIW.

Social Injustices and Racism

Another discouraging aspect of mass incarceration is the injustice you will witness. Not everyone who says they are innocent of their crime, and should therefore not be in prison, is telling the truth. However, some incarcerated people are totally innocent of the crimes for which they are charged, held, and even convicted. And there are some people who are incarcerated as a result of unjust laws. The system is not always, or even usually, fair. As Christians who are wanting to minister the love of God, the wrongness of this can be so jarring as to shake some people's faith in the entire democratic system.

Some persons cope with this by creating a false dichotomy, by making an arbitrary division between the purposes of the judicial system in the U.S. and the responsibilities of Christians doing ministry. On the one hand, since, as was discussed at length in Chapter 7, the current system of incarceration in the U.S. is a failed experiment of the church, those doing ministry do have a responsibility for the failure of that system. But, on the other hand, over-involvement with individual cases can result in ministry worker burnout. And the institution's reaction to a volunteer's overt resistance to the status quo may well be to disallow that person's entry.

The reality of racial injustice is also more difficult to overlook for those who are involved in prison ministry, especially when ministering within jails and prisons. It is difficult to ignore that the proportion of white people inside is smaller and the gravity of their cases overall is greater than minorities, and this is true for both men and women. Racial tensions can run high, more especially in male institutions, where it is the prison itself that insists upon racial segregation.

Mental Illness

Mental illness is a complicating issue that spans our entire expanded definition of prison ministry. And the mentally ill are disproportionately represented in our prisons and jails. Mental illness is far too expansive a topic for me to deal with in-depth in this workbook. I will limit myself to sharing a few experiences from my years of ministering in the prison psychiatric unit.

For example, I was leading a weekly bible study in the psych unit and we were working out way through 1 Timothy. And then we got to this verse: Now unto the King eternal, immortal, invisible, the only wise God, be honour and glory for ever and ever. Amen (1 Tim. 1:17, KJV). (By the way, although most of the women there read one of the new easy-to-read Bible translations, they wanted me to use King James Version because, to some of them, it had more authority as the "real" Bible.) So, I explained the concepts of a God who is eternal and immortal with no problems. But when I got to the description of God as invisible, three out of five women in my study, who suffered from severe schizophrenia, adamantly swore that they saw God all the time. It would have been neither loving nor wise to confront this shared belief. So, I thanked them for their sharing while explaining that, to most people, God really was invisible.

Another time, I was escorting and assisting a team who were presenting a sermon that had gone over very well at their home church and which the pastor then decided to share with our congregation in the psychiatric unit. This sermon included a role-play activity wherein members of the congregation stood in for various Bible characters. The pastor started pointing to women in the congregations saying "You are Moses. And you are Abraham. And you are Sarah." He went through a whole list, appointing these roles indiscriminately. What he did not understand, and refused to hear my cautionary advice about, is that these were mentally ill women struggling to maintain very tenuous holds on reality, and he was telling them to let go. As it was, we already observed regular arguments between the two women who each believed that SHE was the authentic Virgin Mary! I was forced to report this to the staff Chaplain, who never allowed this team to enter the psychiatric unit again, and eventually disallowed them from ministering at the prison.

Finally, church services were often held in the prison psychiatric unit's common room (TV room), and the women were free to come and go. It was not uncommon for it to happen that, while I was preaching a sermon or leading prayer in the front of the room, there would be a woman pacing back and forth in the back of the room, arguing with entities that no one else could see or hear. Outside volunteer ministers usually would take this as unwelcome disruption and distraction to the church service. I learned to see it otherwise. I was honored by her presence.

First of all, I realized that this woman had made a deliberate decision to come to church, to enter into the sacred space where she was exposed to the presence of the Holy Spirit. Secondly, her argument with the voices was very likely because she was trying to get them to be quiet, to leave her alone, so that she could hear the sermon. Thirdly, the fact that she was pacing the back of the room meant that she was trying to be respectful. It was her way of causing as little disruption as possible while still participating in church.

How did I come to reframe her behavior in these terms? I listened to her. I overheard her side of the arguments with the voices. While her words often came out in jumbles that mirrored the disorganization in her brain, some of those words stood alone: "afraid," "kill," "pain," but also "Jesus," and "help." I spent time with her, building a relationship of sorts. I would dare to call it friendship. I learned to recognize in her the *imago dei* (that is, the image of God) in which persons diagnosed with schizophrenia, too, are created.

"No Better Than Prisoners"

Another complicating issue is that those who advocate for prisoners are often seen as "no better than prisoners." This is particularly true of family and friends, who are quick to notice staff's attitudes. Unfortunately, there is a basic presumption amongst many (not all!) staff that everyone in prison or jail lies, cheats, steals, and manipulates without compunction. And this unfortunate and unfair attitude often spills over onto the families and friends who come to prison or jails as visitors.[12]

There is also a suspicion by many custody staff that volunteers are just naïve "do-gooders" who do not understand how dangerous prisoners are, a suspicion that is not always unwarranted. However, on a practical level, the downside is that as ministry volunteers, you may not be granted the credibility, cooperation, and assistance that that you would expect in any other milieu. The upside is that you might be able to turn your interactions into an opportunity for you to minister to correctional staff, another outreach that is well within the scope of my definition of prison ministry for two reasons. First, staff are humans in need of Jesus' love. Second, by ministering to staff, you are improving the conditions for those who they are holding in custody.

Boundaries

I cannot emphasize enough how important it is to understand and maintain healthy boundaries when ministering to incarcerated people. As long as a person is either incarcerated or under the care of an institution, paroles, probation, or program, your relationship with that person is one of unequal power. And YOU are the one with power. Whether you like it or not, whether you are comfortable with it or not, whether it is fair or not, you are still the one with power. And power affects relationship.

If you are ministering within an institution, most prisoners are going to tell you what you want to hear. They have to. You have power and they do not. If there is a misunderstanding, it is the prisoner who will pay the higher cost. If physical boundaries are crossed, you will only lose your privilege to enter the institution, while the prisoner will receive disciplinary documentation, loss of privileges, and usually an increased level of security, all of which will usually delay the release of the prisoner.

I have personally witnessed, and experienced, the devastation that can arise from crossing these boundaries inappropriately. While I was incarcerated, I had one

---

[12] Nell Bernstein has written a sobering book about the way that children of prisoners are often treated as second class citizens, (2005) *All Alone In The World: Children of the Incarcerated.* NY, NY: The New Press.

prison ministry volunteer propose marriage. But the inequality of the power structure made any resulting relationship unhealthy and actually abusive, even though this was not the intent. Alternatively, I also developed appropriate relationships with volunteer ministers and had some of these continue after my release from prison. And, because we carefully respected boundaries while I was incarcerated, it increased our trust in each other so that there are several women who have now become as close to me as my family, in an integrative way.

Maintaining Balance

It is important that ministry volunteers maintain balance and appropriate boundaries, which is not as simple a matter as it sounds. On the one hand, custody staff and police will generally tell you to trust no one and share no personal information. However, this is not the best way to bring the gospel message.

And yet it is true that some people you minister to will be out to use you. You cannot afford to be naïve about this. Prisoners are master manipulators… we have to be in order to survive in prison. Manipulation is not necessarily a negative thing; most people try to put on their best face and behave in a way that gets them what they want.

You need to remember; love does not equal trust. It is entirely possible to love someone without trusting that person. Actually, Jesus understands and accepts us where we are, even when we are too wounded and unhealed to be trustworthy, and then loves us into the kingdom of God.

You will be disappointed. People will lie, or they will not follow through, go back to prison or jail, or not be released when they should be. This can result in burnout: I have seen it happen. I have vivid memories of one ministry volunteer who regularly came to the CIW psychiatric unit in the 1980s. She was devastated by the emotional pain of the prisoners, and then she held on to that pain too personally. She actually had an emotional breakdown during service one Sunday. I remember holding her in my arms as she sobbed uncontrollably while others went to get staff assistance. She needed to be escorted out of the institution and receive mental healthcare and could never return.

Staying Safe

Some criminals are truly dangerous. Being redeemable does not mean that everyone will accept redemption. Some sociopathic persons in prison will do and say anything to get what they want, and they can be compelling. You will not always determine who is sincere and who is out to use or abuse you. So how do you keep yourself and vulnerable others safe?

People diagnosed as pedophiles have extremely low (or nil) cure rates, and yet may be sincere in their faith and need for church. What can you do to balance the very real spiritual needs of persons convicted of sex crimes with your very real need to protect the members of your church? A friend of mine in ministry shared that it makes him sad to know that one developmentally disabled gentleman with a sex crime record wants to go to church, but knows that "no one is gonna sit next to me."

Even the sincerest Christ-following persons who are struggling with drug and alcohol addictions are vulnerable to relapse, especially during times of extreme stress. Further, while sobriety may be more easily accomplished during incarceration due to the strict control of that environment, the challenges facing persons released from custody can be overwhelming. These people are in desperate need of fellowship and support from the church. How do you meet these needs and yet protect yourself and the church from financial and property loss?

There are no easy answers to these questions. But these are questions that those involved in any aspect of prison ministry must confront.

Not all prison ministry is equally unsafe. Those whose ministry is being a pen pal to an incarcerated person are much less physically vulnerable than those who enter prisons and jails, but are still vulnerable to manipulation if good personal boundaries have not been established. Likewise, there is a much greater risk to the members of the church where formerly incarcerated persons are welcomed into the local congregation than when ministry occurs somewhere else off the church campus. You will need to seriously consider how to respond to whatever call God is making on you.

It is an error to be so afraid that you cannot accept God's call. If God is calling you, he also has the power to protect you. But we must still be wise (Matt. 10:16).

Patience or Persistence:

It is not easy to maintain a balance between being patient and being persistent. Bureaucracies never, ever, move quickly! However, it takes wisdom and discernment to determine whether you should be pushing or waiting. Is your paperwork being processed slowly, or has it been lost entirely? Has staff truly forgotten your request, or is your request slowly moving up in a long queue of priorities and the chain of command? I cannot tell you how to handle these situations; each one is unique. But I can promise you that, if you are doing prison ministry, these are questions you will face and need to answer.

Discouragement: How do you keep from getting discouraged? Prison ministry can be thrillingly fulfilling, seeing God's salvation work coming to fruition in the lives of those who have been imprisoned and those around them. However, there will be heart-rending disappointments. There will be those who, as in the parable of the sower and seeds (Matt. 13:1-9, 18-23), will receive Jesus with their whole heart, and then turn away due to the difficulties of life. There will be those who are simply being manipulative and are using and abusing others. Sometimes those who you minister to, people who have made life changing commitments to Jesus, do not outlive their incarceration.

I know firsthand how devastating it was for those who were ministering to me when, time after time, God granted the miraculous answer to prayers and I was found suitable for parole, only to have that granting overturned by the governor. This happened ten times from 1989 to 2009. Finally in 2010, my eleventh parole grant was allowed to stand and I was released.

As in any other spiritual calling, it is important to remained centered in God, to remember that this is God's ministry, God's mission, God's work, and we are only his instruments. We do not know how many ways our obedient work has been used by God to minister his love and his will.

Denominations

"I was whatever denomination that my chaplain was." Although I usually say it with a laugh, it is true. In my 30 years of incarceration, our Protestant chaplains ranged from Presbyterian to American Baptist to Pentecostal to African Methodist Episcopal (AME). And although I saw subtle differences in how our prison church was being shaped, I really had no idea of the significance of various denominations. Meanwhile, although our chaplain would be from some particular denomination, the various volunteer groups, many of which carried over from one chaplaincy term to the next, were of various denominations. And then, to further cloud the picture, the volunteer team members were specifically prohibited from saying anything against any other denomination. One chaplain explained to me during an interview (after my release from prison) that, due to the mandate for freedom of religious expression, she

"Approved" for Parole Does Not Mean "Released"

A friend of mine, a pastor, just sent me a text message, "The LORD has spoken…Sheila's parole hearing was successful!!! She was APPROVED for parole. Hallelujah, Hallelujah, Hallelujah!! Next step, she'll be released after a 4-month wait to allow the governor to approve or deny the Board's decision! It's just a matter of time…" This is awesome and joyous news. It is a miracle indeed. We have been working together for months to help Sheila and her family prepare for this day. I hated having to put a damper on it.

I replied, "Actually, in California, it's a 4 month wait to ensure there were no procedural mistakes in the hearing. If, and only if, her parole suitability is confirmed by the Decision Review Board at the end of the 4 months wait, her paperwork will be sent to the Governor's office to give him the opportunity to veto the decision. Our current governor has been pretty good about not abusing his veto power too much."

She responded, "It makes me think about what you have said about the struggle you have gone through in this coming out of pandemic time…we are there but not there yet. We want to be hopeful, but not wanting to be too hopeful."

"Exactly! We learn to just appreciate that this is good news, but not actually trust too much. Hopefully, Sheila will get out this first time through and not be so deeply wounded. It was 11 times for me. It was 7 times for my cellmate Martina. Our friend Lisa is on round 4. It's a brutal system."

"Argh! That makes me angry," she texted back.

"Yeah, it should make you angry. And it is not just the prisoner who pays. The family and loved one also go through incredible stress. Imagine what it was like for my parents, all those times of hoping and waiting. One ministry volunteer shared with me that she went through a real 'crisis of faith' trying to come to terms with the situation. There are a lot of hidden victims in this system."

felt required to ask all volunteers to refrain from mentioning their denominational affiliations.

The ecumenical mindedness that results is very positive. There is very little conflict between denominations. However, prisoners who have not been affiliated with any particular denomination prior to their incarceration generally have no idea about what makes a denomination or what that signifies. This lack of knowledge, in turn, makes it difficult for former prisoners to choose a church that suits their spiritual needs outside of the prison context. And this leads to dissatisfaction and even discouragement for newly released prisoners who are looking for a new home church.

Attitudes About Prison

Even with ministries that do not enter prisons and jails, sometimes even in prayer groups at churches, not everyone is convinced that prisoners are human or redeemable. This can be tricky ground to negotiate.

I once served on a church council with a man who had worked in law enforcement, and further, had a close family member who was in prison. While making the clear point that he was not referring to me, he declared that "NOT all prisoners are redeemable!" Certainly, not all prisoners accept redemption in Christ. But for persons who have been sufficiently hurt or frightened, they may have a very difficult time conceptualizing that Christ died even for those who refuse him. However, as we discussed in Chapter 2, Jesus died for Barabbas who, to our knowledge, showed no remorse.

AA/NA: Alcoholics Anonymous (AA) and Narcotics Anonymous (NA) are very high profile in jails and prisons. Anyone doing prison ministry needs to have a basic awareness of what these groups are, how they are utilized within the criminal justice system, and what kinds of attitudes prevail about AA/NA.

Alcohol and drug use are associated with a high percentage of the crimes for which people are incarcerated. Sometimes, the actual use of the substance is deemed criminal. Sometimes crimes are committed in order to obtain drugs or alcohol. And sometimes crimes are committed by persons who are under the influence of alcohol or drugs. Thus, almost every locked facility invites AA/NA representatives and/or holds meetings.

Some Christians object to the basic premises of AA. Their objections usually fall into one of two categories: that acknowledging a "Higher Power" does not directly honor Jesus, or that deliverance from addiction is conferred when one accepts Jesus as savior. I suggest that both of these objections are based on misunderstanding or misinformation about AA/NA. Firstly, AA/NA was conceptualized and originated by Christians. The term "higher power" is used instead of "God" or "Jesus" in order to initially make the program accessible for those who are not Christians. However, I have met many, many people who have had amazing conversion experiences when they realized that the "higher power" is indeed named Jesus! Secondly, although it is absolutely true that for some people, salvation and deliverance from addiction occur simultaneously, this is not the process for most of the people I know. Healing is often a process, and sometimes a slow and painful process. AA/NA can make a huge difference in this process.

Personally, I cannot speak highly enough of AA and all of its associated groups. While in prison, I volunteered as a co-facilitator for a Christian 12 Steps for Co-Dependency group. Because I paroled to a sober-living home, even though I had no alcohol or drug background or restrictions, I was still mandated by the halfway house to attend AA five days a week. The support, life lessons, and friendships I found there are ongoing in my life ten years later.

Discussion Questions

1. Which of these complicating issues are you surprised by? Why?

2. When you become discouraged, as you undoubtedly sometimes will be, what steps will you take to help you keep from getting bitter?

3. What kind of boundaries can be maintained that will allow you to fully integrate those affected by mass incarceration into your church without risking the safety of vulnerable church members?

4. This chapter states that "Some chaplains are very good, some are very bad, and some are simply ineffective." How do you think this might relate to Power Dyad Theory categories? Why?

5. What are your views about AA/NA? How might those views impact how you minister to people struggling with addictions?

Chapter 12

What the Incarcerated Give Back (or What's in it for the Church?)

Participating in prison ministry is a matter of "enlightened self-interest" for most churches. What do I mean? It is in the best interest of the church to meet the needs of people involved with mass incarceration. There are two reasons for this. First, it is good for the spiritual health of the local church body. Secondly, people involved in mass incarceration have a lot to offer the church.

Spiritual Health of the Local Church

A church that only hears the perspectives of others who are just like them is a church in danger of becoming ineffective at mission, or worse, of veering dangerously distant from gospel truths. What my mother says of individuals is also true of churches, that "No one ever wakes up one morning and says, 'Gee, I think I'll ruin the rest of my life today.'" But churches can become so insulated from the realities around them that they become ineffectual at ministering "to the least of these" (Matt. 25:45).

It is good for the spiritual health of the church to have a more realistic understanding of what the Bible refers to as freedom. As the "Shelter in Place" and "Safer at Home" restrictions of the COVID19 pandemic changed the lives of so many of us in the U.S., I regularly heard or read about people who were comparing lockdown to being in prison or jail. I certainly understand that people were feeling overwhelmed and imposed upon, that they were having difficulty adjusting to so many new restrictions, and that they were fearing for their personal safety. However, many who were comparing these experiences to prison were doing so from a sense of entitlement, from frustration arising from the belief that free Americans should not have to be "locked in." In both cases, gaining a perspective of what being in prison or jail really entails provides a reality check. It answers the questions that many of my friends and loved ones began asking me about how to maintain a "cup half full" optimism in such a situation.

What kind of practical advice does prison provide about living in close quarters? It is not easy when we cannot get away from each other. Living two to a cell was one of the most difficult challenges of prison. However, even a very small home has more space per person than a seven-foot by nine-foot prison cell. We learned to give one another what we called "bunkie space."[13] We discovered that it is not selfish to insist upon a block of time in which each person can be private. This may mean that, for a half hour a day while I am doing my devotionals, I refuse to talk or interact with my bunkie. The lesson here is that it is absolutely alright to be annoyed and disenchanted with those we love and/or live with sometimes. Those who have survived real

Sermonette: Freedom 'from' and freedom 'to'

Freedom does not always mean "freedom from." Freedom also means "freedom to." Christian "freedom from" means freedom from being forced to follow our sinful and selfish nature. This is not at all the same as freedom from prison or freedom from the cares and troubles of our life. Paul specifically reminds us that "'All things are lawful,' but not all things are beneficial. 'All things are lawful,' but not all things build up. Do not seek your own advantage, but that of the other" (1 Cor. 10:23-24). Jesus did not promise to deliver us from all of our problems; He did, however, promise to be with us during all of them.

In the meanwhile, Jesus gives us the "freedom to" love one another. Gal. 5:13 says "For you were called to freedom, brothers and sisters; only do not use your freedom as an opportunity for self-indulgence, but through love become slaves to one another." In prison, I love as a countercultural act of rebellion. "You can't make me not love you, no matter who you are!" I am free to love. I am free to pray for my family knowing that prayer brings the presence of God into whatever situation I am praying over.

---

[13] "Bunkie" is the term I heard used most often at CIW for the person who sleeps on the same bunk bed. "Cellie" is a term that is also used, but more often for those who share a multi-bunk cell.

adversity can be a resource for the church in just such times of wider spread adversity.

It is good for the spiritual health of the church to be reminded that ministry is ALWAYS a two-way street. It can be humbling, and sometimes difficult to accept, this realization that those we minister to also minister to us. However, the truth is that it is not uncommon for prisoners who meet Jesus in prison to throw themselves into life of studying the Bible. Their fervor and dedication to study may outpace many seminary students, and may in fact lead to seminary classes and degrees. I was not the only formerly incarcerated person studying at Fuller Theological Seminary as I completed my doctoral work there.

It is good for the spiritual health of the church to be challenged theologically about redemption. As we discussed in Chapters 9, redemption is the most essential biblical gift for prisoners. Yet there are many in our churches who do not live as if Christ's redemption extends to all persons. There is value for those to see Jesus' redemptive work alive in the persons of those who were or are incarcerated.

As I look at my own ordination and how people have reacted to it, most often God is given glory for having redeemed me from domestic abuse and incarceration. If God has redeemed someone as sinful as me and my incarcerated brothers and sisters, then God really can and will redeem members of his church who hold private knowledge of their own sins.

It is good for the spiritual health of the church to be reminded to live in a spirit of abundance. I find that the people I meet in churches outside prison are much richer, in myriad ways, than they realize. Many people are looking at themselves and their world from a position of scarcity rather than a place of abundance. What I mean by this is that I see an underlying sense of entitlement that results in the church looking at what it is lacking rather than what God has already provided. This is expressed as "We need more resources in order to do what we are called to do" when, in reality, God has already provided more than enough resources. "What we are called to do" may be as simple as living joyfully and lovingly. I have watched with a full heart as the homeless men at a local Lutheran mission, many of whom have been incarcerated, place pocket change in their collection plate during their church service. Just as heartwarming is that the collection plate is then counted and processed after the service by one of their own. These men, who are often the object of scorn, teach us what the parable of the widow's mite really means (Mark 12:41-44, Luke 21:1-4).

During a recent interview, a committee member asked how it is that I "endured the claustrophobia of being shut up in that dark and lonely place, and found light there?" The man asking this question admitted that he was referencing his own reactions to the Covid-19 restrictions, since he was struggling against darkness and claustrophobia.

I couldn't help but laugh, to his surprise. But as I explained, "First, being locked in that prison cell was not necessarily a bad thing. It also meant that the world was locked out. Secondly, Jesus was locked in there with me and my cellmate Martina. We had the Light living in our cell with us! How could we need anything more?"

He responded, "Well, you have certainly given us a new perspective! I am going to have to think about that." A glimpse into the reality of prison shifted his thinking from what he did not have, in terms of usual freedom of movement and personal contact with loved ones, to what he did have: a relationship with Jesus that no circumstance or situation can limit.

Another way this thinking from a perspective of abundance shows itself is in gift giving. In our commercial society in the U.S., many people worry about whether the gifts they are giving are expensive enough to be appreciated and admired. In prison, where personal possessions were so limited, and access to goods was very restricted, any gift at all was a sacrifice. I have seen grown women cry over a two-cent Tootsie Roll candy! Regifted items, gifts that were not quite new, grocery items, gift certificates for a personal service, or even just a pencil, are all treasured inside.

From birth and until we became roommates, Martina had lived a life based on scarcity. Now she lives a life of abundance. The circumstances had nothing to do with it. Martina may live amongst the very poorest of the poor in a barrio in Tijuana, but one of the sisters in the church gave her a birthday gift this year, "*a fresh potato! I ate it for supper!*" Our prison experience taught us how rich we are, a lesson that stays with us.

We want to contribute! Those who find salvation and redemption in Christ while incarcerated are often especially eager to pay back for what we have taken from society. We are motivated to become part of the solution instead of being the problem.

What we Have to Offer

Leadership: Strangely enough, many of us found out in prison that we could be leaders. Further many of us learn how to lead from the bottom, without abusing power. True, prison breeds and encourages some bullies who lead by violence and coercion. But prison church leaders are provided an opportunity to learn to lead through love and wisdom.

I was invited to a neighborhood barbeque at our mayor's home a couple of years ago due to my involvement in local urban gardening as a response to food insecurity. In this moderate sized group of local people who are active in our community (perhaps 150 people in all), I met up with two other people who had also served life-term sentences in California prisons. Between the three of us we had served more than 80 years. And here we were at the mayor's house, having transitioned from prisoners to community leaders.

We are one body: The church is made more whole when its members' needs are met. It is ultimately good for the church when its parts are integrated.

Martin Luther King Jr. called 11 a.m. on Sunday morning "the most segregated hour in America." Traditionally, church congregations are mainly monochromatic. However, this is not the case in many prisons. At CIW, we all shared one Interfaith Chapel: Black, white, Hispanic, Protestant, Catholic, Muslim, Jew. And, for many of us, the segregation in the churches outside feels false and contrived. So, for churches who are struggling with how to make their congregations more diverse, former prisoners are often experienced in how to extend welcome to diverse others.

Richness of life experience: As we have discussed at depth about Muted Group Theory, subdominant group members have life experiences that are different and not readily explainable to the dominant group. But when a church embraces subdominant group members, including former prisoners, those persons bring new perspectives. Prisoners have experienced aspects of life that can enrich the church.

This year my pastor's Lenten sermons focused on finding light in the darkness. For Palm Sunday, I was therefore asked to share "lessons from the darkness" with the congregation. After all, where it is darkest is where the light shines the brightest.

Those who have been incarcerated can also bring new perspectives on God's grace and redemption. Prisoners can provide new depths of meaning to Christian worship clichés such as "free from bondage," "released from shackles," and being a "new creations in Christ." We remind the church of joys it might otherwise overlook by appreciating God's small mercies.

Healing: It is easier for victims to receive healing when the victimizer takes responsibility for hurtful actions. But this means there must be an interaction of some sort between perpetrator and victim, even if this is a surrogate relationship. This is what many restorative justice programs are trying to foster (We talked about restorative justice in chapters 7 and 10).

One way this can work is when someone owns the way that their actions have hurt and affected others, admits the ways that they have victimized others, and then sincerely apologizes. The apology does not necessarily have to be made only to the actual victim, but may be extended to surrogate victims, those who have been violated similarly by a different person. This kind of healing experience can be very effective at providing closure to a victim.

A pivotal point in my own healing had to do with an apology I received from a prison ministry volunteer who had never directly harmed me. The late Jeff Fenholt, who played the title role in the original Broadway production and tour of "Jesus Christ Superstar," came as a guest speaker to CIW while I was incarcerated. He shared his testimony in brutal detail, which included his abusing drugs, alcohol, and ultimately his wife. And then, with tears streaming down his face, he apologized. Not only did he apologize for abusing his wife, he apologized to us, to me. He took responsibility for, and apologized for, the physical and emotional abuse that each of us in the audience had received at the hands of others. This was an important milestone on my personal journey of healing; accepting Jeff's apology was the first step in my learning to forgive the wrongs that had been done to me. Since those who abused me have all died without apologizing or taking responsibility, this gesture of Jeff Fenholt's was even more meaningful. Of course, not all present or former prisoners are willing and able to initiate a healing event such as the above. But when given the opportunity, some will, and the church will benefit.

We want healing for our children and for subsequent generations…to stop the "curses of generations."

Sermonette: A New Perspective on a Familiar Scripture

The first sermon I ever preached in prison was based on Jer. 29:4-14. Most of the time I only hear about verses 10-14. But I came to realize that this entire section was God giving directions for how his people were supposed to live while in captivity. The spiritual applications of this scripture are profound.

4 Thus says the Lord of hosts, the God of Israel, to all the exiles whom I have sent into exile from Jerusalem to Babylon: 5 Build houses and live in them; plant gardens and eat what they produce. 6 Take wives and have sons and daughters; take wives for your sons, and give your daughters in marriage, that they may bear sons and daughters; multiply there, and do not decrease. 7 But seek the welfare of the city where I have sent you into exile, and pray to the Lord on its behalf, for in its welfare you will find your welfare. 8 For thus says the Lord of hosts, the God of Israel: Do not let the prophets and the diviners who are among you deceive you, and do not listen to the dreams that they dream, [a] 9 for it is a lie that they are prophesying to you in my name; I did not send them, says the Lord.

10 For thus says the Lord: Only when Babylon's seventy years are completed will I visit you, and I will fulfill to you my promise and bring you back to this place. 11 For surely I know the plans I have for you, says the Lord, plans for your welfare and not for harm, to give you a future with hope. 12 Then when you call upon me and come and pray to me, I will hear you. 13 When you search for me, you will find me; if you seek me with all your heart, 14 I will let you find me, says the Lord, and I will restore your fortunes and gather you from all the nations and all the places where I have driven you, says the Lord, and I will bring you back to the place from which I sent you into exile. (Jer. 29:4-14)

First, there is a certain comfort in realizing that sometimes God's people do end up in captivity. Sometimes it is their own fault for having committed sins, but this is not the case for everyone, just like with prisons. Next, we are told to settle in and be at home there, build a community, while we wait for God's deliverance. We are to plant a garden and harvest the fruit of the Holy Spirit. We are to bear children; generations of spiritual rebirthing is possible and will cause the church to grow. Pray for the place that God has set us in, and that includes praying for our captors and guards. This is our God given home for the time being, and we need to be his living presence here.

Discussion Questions

1. How do you allow those you minister to, to minister back to you?

2. How can the churches outside better connect with the churches inside?

3. In what ways could the sermonette on Jer. 29 inform how you minister to prisoners? How do you honor the special ministries that God has called prisoners to?

4. What gifts can you imagine former or current prisoners being able to share with your church?

Conclusion

Tying Up Some Loose Ends

I sincerely hope that you have found the contents of this book enlightening and practically helpful. In the introduction I claimed that by the time you reach the conclusion of this book you should be able to give thoughtful and informed answers to the following questions.

Please answer these discussion questions again here:

1. Why do you believe that mass incarceration is a topic that is relevant to YOU?

2. What is your definition of prison ministry?

3. What is your understanding of power dynamics and your personal power?

4. What does prison ministry really look like from a Christian perspective?

5. How might God be calling you to participate in prison ministry?

My hope is that you are noticing significant differences from your initial answers to these questions, and that you feel much better prepared to reach out to currently and formerly incarcerated persons and their families with God's love. But my hope goes one step further, that you are now challenged not only to do more effective prison ministry, but that you are rethinking incarceration as a necessary component of our criminal justice system.

I am confounding prison ministry, and new models of criminal justice, because the two have traditionally been inextricable. It is only in the last two hundred years that separation of church and state have caused a false separation of the two. I hesitate to call criminal justice that has resulted in mass incarceration "justice."

Let me make clear that I am not advocating that all criminals should be free to continue behaviors that do not respect the safety, property, and lives of the community. What I am saying is that the incarceration of criminals in prisons, as they exist today, is not meeting the needs of the community and that the model needs to be re-examined. The church needs to take responsibility for having initiated the current model of mass incarceration. And the church needs to come up with an answer, a better model.

Complacency by the church, ignoring or overlooking the proverbial elephant in the room that is mass incarceration, is not an acceptable response. As I stated early on, I do not have all the answers. But I am bringing my questions to you, my brothers and sisters in Christ, so that the body, working together, can develop and implement an intentional new model of how we respond to crime and criminals. How wonderful it would be if the term "prison ministry" were outdated because the church had provided a new model of dealing with criminal behavior that did not rely almost entirely on incarceration.

Bibliography

Acevedo, John Felipe. 2012. 1600 to 1776: Introduction. In *The Social History of Crime and Punishment in America: An Encyclopedia*, edited by Wilbur R. Miller. London: SAGE Publications, Inc.

Anderson, Ray S. 1997. *The Soul of Ministry: Forming Leaders for God's People*. Louisville, KY: Westminster John Knox Press.

Anonymous. 1953. *Twelve Steps and Twelve Traditions*. NY, NY: Alcoholics Anonymous World Services.

Ardener, Shirley. 2005. "Ardener's "Muted Groups": The Genesis of an Idea and its Praxis: ." *Women and Language* 28 (2):50.

Barkman, Linda. 2018.

Barkman, Linda. 2020. Hidden Power & False Expectations: Muted Group Theory for Urban Mission. Skyforest, CA: Urban Loft Publishers.

Bernstein, Nell. 2005. All Alone In The World: Children of the Incarcerated. NY, NY: The New Press.

Blackmon, Douglas A. 2008. Slavery by Another Name: The Re-Enslavement of Black Americans from the Civil War to World War II. New York: Anchor Books.

Bozelko, Chandra. 2020. While the Coronovirus Pandemic Lasts, We Must Stop Filling Prisons or We'll Extend the Crisis. In *Hot Take*: NBC. Retrieved from https://www.nbcnews.com/think/opinion/while-coronavirus-pandemic-lasts-we-must-stop-filling-prisons-or-ncna1162176

Brown, Mark and Stuart Ross. 2010. "Mentoring, Social Capital and Desistance: A Study of Women Released from Prison." *The Australian and New Zealand Journal of Criminology* 43 (1):31-50.

California, State of. 2015. California Code of Regulations. In *Title 15*, edited by California Department of Corrections and Rehabilitation. Sacramento, CA: State of California.

Chapman, David W. 2013. "The Legendary John Howard and Prison Reform in the Eighteenth Century." *The Eighteenth Century* 54 (4 (Winter)):545-550.

Christianson, Scott. 1998. *With Liberty for Some: 500 Years of Impriwsonment in America.* Boston Northeastern University Press.

Criss, Doug. 2018. This is the 30-year old ad everybody is talking about. *CNN Politics.*

Cullen, James. 2018. The History of Mass Incarceration. *Brennan Center for Justice.* Retrieved from https://www.brennancenter.org/our-work/analysis-opinion/history-mass-incarceration

Davis, Angela Y. 2003. *Are Prisons Obsolete?* Toronto, Canada: Publishers Group Canada.

Davis, Angela Y. 2020. Why Arguments Against Abolition Inevitably Fail. *Level.* Accessed July 1, 2021. Retrieved from medium.com website: https://level.medium.com/why-arguments-against-abolition-inevitably-fail-991342b8d042

Davison, Dawn, Valerie Jenness and Mona Lynch. 2011. "Thinking About the Past and Envisioning the Future: A Review Essay of Candace Kruttschnitt and Rosemary Gartner, *Marking Time in the Golden State: Women's Imprisonment in California.*" *Punishment and Society* 13 (2):230-243.

DuVernay, Ava 2016. 13th. Netflicks.

Funes, Yessenia. 2019. California Is Blaming Prison Reform for Incarcerated Fire Fighting Labor Shortage. *Gizmodo: Earther.* Retrieved from https://earther.gizmodo.com/california-is-blaming-prison-reform-for-incarcerated-fi-1837612038

Green, Erica L., Mark Walker and Eliza Shapiro. 2020. "A Battle for the Souls of Black Girls." *New York Times,* October 1, 2020. https://www.nytimes.com/2020/10/01/us/politics/black-girls-school-discipline.html?utm_source=pocket-newtab.

Halliday, Stephen. 2006. *Newgate: London's Prototype of Hell.* Stroud, Gloucestershire, UK: Sutton Publishing Ltd.

Harris, Heather; Justin Gross, Joseph Hayes, and Alexandria Gumbs. 2019. Just the FACTS: California's Prison Population. *Public Policy Institute of California.* Retrieved from https://www.ppic.org/publication/californias-prison-population/

Hofstede, Geert. 2009. "Dimensionalizing Cultures: the Hofstede Model in contest." In *Intercultural Communication: A Reader, 13th ed.*, edited by Larry A. Samovar, Richard E. Porter, and Edwin R. McDaniel. Boston, MA: Wadsworth Cengage Learning.

Jweied, Maha. 2014. Expert Working Group Report: Native American Traditional Justice Practices. edited by U. S. Department of Justice & U.S. Department of the Interior.

Kahn, Drew. 2019. "5 Facts Behind America's High Incarceration Rate." CNN, accessed April 21.

Kearney, Milissa S., Benjamin H. Harris, Elisa Jacome, and Lucie Parker. 2014. "Ten Economic Facts about Crime and Incarceration in the United States." *The Hamilton Project*.

Kenny, Paula and Liam Leonard. 2014. *The Sustainability of Restorative Justice.* Vol. 14, *Advances in Sustainability and Environmental Jusice.* Bingley, UK: Emerald Group Publishing Limited.

Killian, Gloria and Sandra Kobrin. 2012. *Full Circle: A True Story of Murder, Lies, and Vindication.* Far Hills, NJ: New Horizon Press.

Kitzinger, Celia and Alison Thomas. 1995. *Sexual Harrasment: A Discursive Approach.* Edited by Sue Wilkinson and Celia Kitzinger, *Gender and psychology: Feminist and critical perspectives.* . Thousand Oaks, CA: SAGE Publications.

Koschmann, Matthew A. and Brittany L. Peterson. 2013. "Rethinking Recidivism: A Communication Approach to Prisoner Reentry." *Journal of Applied Social Science* 7 (22):188-207.

LaHurd, Carol Schersten. 2013. "When was it that we saw you sick or in prison and visited you?". *Dialog* 52 (2):87-90.

Lee, Hedwig; McCormick, Tyler; Hicken, Margaret T.; and Wildeman, Christopher. 2015. Racial Inequalities in Connectedness to Imprisoned Individuals in the United States. *Cambridge Core.* Accessed July 1, 2021. Retrieved from https://www.cambridge.org/core/journals/du-bois-review-social-science-research-on-race/article/abs/racial-inequalities-in-connectedness-to-imprisoned-individuals-in-the-united-states/D015904ED108B3B0A18454450104845A

Lee, Morgan. 2019. Prison Was My First Pulpit. *Christianity Today*. Retrieved from https://www.christianitytoday.com/ct/2019/january-web-only/prison-first-pulpit-domestic-violence-incarceration.html

Levad, Amy. 2011. ""I Was in Prison and You Visited Me": A Sacramental Approach to Rehabilitative and Restorative Criminal Justice." *Journal of the Society of Christian Ethics* 31 (2):93-112. doi: 10.2307/23562919.

Liebmann, Marian. 2007. *Restorative Justice: How It Works*. London, UK: Jessica Kingsley Publishers.

McBride, Jennifer M. 2014. "Christ Existing as Concrete Community Today." *Theology Today* 71 (1):92-105. doi: 10.1177/0040573613518548.

Meares, Mary, Annette Torres, Denise Derkacs, John Oetzel, and Tamar Ginossar. 2004. "Employee mistreatment and muted voices in the culturally diverse workplace." *Journal of Applied Communication Research* 32 (1):4-27.

Melton, Ada Pecos. 2005. "Indigenous Justice Systems and Tribal Society." In *Justice as Healing: Indigenous Ways. Writings of Community Peacemaking and Restorative Justice from the Native Law Centre*, edited by Wanda D. McCaslin, 108-120. St. Paul, NM: Living Justice Press.

Merriam-Webster On-line Dictionary. (2015). Retrieved from https://www.merriam-webster.com/dictionary/hospitality?utm_campaign=sd&utm_medium=serp&utm_source=jsonld

M2W2 Ministries. (2019). Match 2. accessed March 21, 2021. Retrieved from http://m2w2.org/

Nelson, Derek. 2013. "With liberty and some justice for a few: thinking theologically about criminal justice." *Dialog* 52 (2):93-98.

Schmid, M. 2003. ""The Eye of God": Religious Beliefs and Punishment in Early Nineteenth-Century Prison Reform." *Theology Today* 59 (4):546-558.

Sexton, Jason S. 2015. "Toward a prison theology of California's ecclesia incarcerate." *Theology* 118 (2):83-91. doi: 10.1177/0040571x14559159.

Stevenson, Bryan. 2015. *Just Mercy*. New York: Spiegel and Grau.

Union, American Civil Liberties. 2019. "Mass Incarceration." accessed May 19. https://www.aclu.org/issues/smart-justice/mass-incarceration.

Vargas, Alicia. 2013. "Who ministers to whom: Matthew 25:31-46 and prison ministry." *Dialog* 52 (2):128-137.

Waldrep, Christopher. 2011. "On Violence in the South: Criminal Justice through the Civil Rights Era." University of Mississippi.

Williams, R. L. (2013). A thicker Jesus as a contextual and embodied Christian ethics. *Perspectives in Religious Studies*, 40(2), 155-166.

Zernova, Margarita. 2007. Restorative Justice: Ideals and Realities, International and Comparative Criminal Justice. New York, NY: Routledge.

Made in the USA
Monee, IL
21 June 2022

98396109R00095

Made in the USA
Monee, IL
21 June 2022